GERMAN
in 10 minutes a day®

by Kristine Kershul, M.A., University of California, Santa Barbara

Consultants: Susan Worthington, Jessie G. McGuire

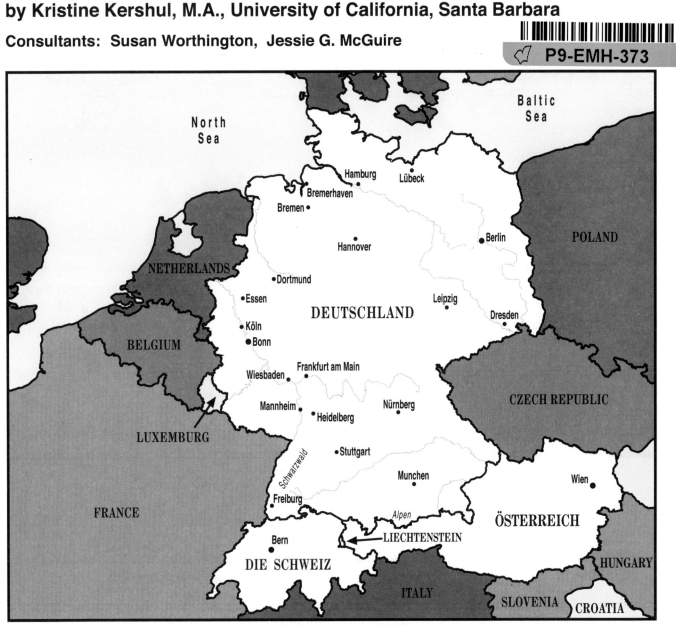

Bilingual Books, Inc.
1719 West Nickerson Street, Seattle, WA 98119
Tel: (206) 284-4211 Fax: (206) 284-3660
www.10minutesaday.com • www.bbks.com

ISBN-13: 978-1-931873-03-1   First printing, February 2009

Can you say this?

(vahs)   *(ist)*   *(dahs)*
Was ist das?
what   is   that

(dahs)   *(ein)*   *(ice)*
Das ist ein Eis.
an   ice-cream cone

(veer)   *(murk-ten)*   *(ein)*   *(ice)*
Wir möchten ein Eis.
we   would like

If you can say this, you can learn to speak German. You will be able to easily order wine, lunch, theater tickets, pastry, or anything else you wish. With your best German accent you simply ask „**Was ist das?**" *(vahs) (ist) (dahs)* and, upon learning what it is, you can order it with „**Wir möchten das**" *(veer) (murk-ten) (dahs)*. Sounds easy, doesn't it?

The purpose of this book is to give you an **immediate** speaking ability in German. German is spoken not only in Germany, but in Switzerland and Austria as well. Using the acclaimed *"10 minutes a day*®*"* methodology, you will acquire a large working vocabulary that will suit your needs, and you will acquire it almost automatically. To aid you, this book offers a unique and easy system of pronunciation above each word which walks you through learning German.

If you are planning a trip or moving to where German is spoken, you will be leaps ahead of everyone if you take just a few minutes a day to learn the easy key words that this book offers. Start with Step 1 and don't skip around. Each day work as far as you can comfortably go in those 10 minutes. Don't overdo it. Some days you might want to just review. If you forget a word, you can always look it up in the glossary. Spend your first 10 minutes studying the map on the previous page. And yes, have fun learning your new language.

As you work through the Steps, always use the special features which only this series offers. This book contains sticky labels and flash cards, free words, puzzles, and quizzes. When you have completed the book, cut out the menu guide and take it along on your trip.

(dahs) *(ahl-fah-bate)*

Das Alphabet
the   alphabet

Above all new words is an easy pronunciation guide. Many German letters are pronounced just as they are in English, however, others are pronounced quite differently. Practice these sounds with the examples given which are mostly towns or areas in Europe which you might visit. Refer to this Step whenever you need help, but remember, spend no longer than 10 minutes a day.

German letter	English sound	Examples	Write it here
a	ah	**A**lpen *(ahl-pen)* Alps	_____
ä	ay	**D**änemark *(day-nuh-mark)* Denmark	_____
au	ow / au	Pass**au** *(pahs-sau)*	_____
äu	oy	Allg**äu** *(ahl-goy)*	_____
b	b	**B**asel *(bah-zel)*	_____
***ch** *(varies)*	*(breathe hard)* H=hk / h / k	Aa**ch**en *(ah-Hen)*	_____
	sh	Mün**ch**en *(mewn-shen)*	_____
d	d	**D**ortmund *(dort-moont)*	_____
e *(varies)*	ay eh	Br**e**m**e**n *(bray-men)*	_____
e *(end of word)*	uh	Elb**e** *(el-buh)*	_____
ei	eye / ai / i / y	**Ei**ger *(eye-gair)*	_____
er	air	B**er**lin *(bair-leen)*	_____
eu	oy	**Eu**ropa *(oy-roh-pah)*	_____
f	f	**F**rankfurt *(frahnk-foort)*	_____
g *(as in good)*	g	**G**enf *(genf)* Geneva	_____
h	h	**H**essen *(hes-sen)*	_____
i	ih / ee	**I**nnsbruck *(ins-brook)*	_____
ie	ee	K**ie**l *(keel)*	_____
j	y	**J**ura *(yoo-rah)*	_____

* This sound varies even among German speakers. The "H" is to help you remember to breathe hard while pronouncing an "hk" sound or even a gutteral "h." This will be your trickiest sound in German, but practice, practice, practice and you will master it.

German Letter	English Sound	Example	Write it here
k	k	**K**onstanz *(kohn-stahnts)*	_____
l	l	**L**übeck *(lew-beck)*	_____
m	m	**M**annheim *(mahn-hime)*	_____
n	n	**N**euschwanstein *(noy-shvahn-shtine)* castle in southern Germany	_____
o	oh	**O**berammergau *(oh-bair-ah-mair-gau)*	_____
ö	ur / uhr	**Ö**sterreich *(ur-stair-ry-sh)* Austria	_____
p	p	**P**otsdam *(pohts-dahm)*	_____
qu	kv	Mar**qu**artstein *(mar-kvart-shtine)*	_____
r	r *(slightly rolled)*	**R**ostock *(roh-shtohk)*	_____
s *(varies)*	s	Wie**s**baden *(vees-bah-den)*	_____
	z	Dre**s**den *(drayz-den)*	_____
sch	sh	**Sch**weiz *(shvites)*	_____
sp	shp	**Sp**eyer *(shpy-air)*	_____
ß / ss	ss / s	Me**ß**stetten *(mess-shtet-ten)*	_____
st	sht	**St**uttgart *(shtoot-gart)*	_____
t	t	**T**irol *(tee-rohl)*	_____
th	t	**Th**un *(toon)*	_____
u	oo	**U**lm *(oolm)*	_____
ü	ew / ue	D**ü**sseldorf *(dew-sel-dorf)*	_____
v	f	**V**orarlberg *(for-arl-bairg)*	_____
w	v	**W**ien *(veen)* Vienna	_____
x	ks	Cu**x**haven *(kooks-hah-fen)*	_____
y	oo	S**y**lt *(soolt)*	_____
z	ts	Koblen**z** *(koh-blents)*	_____

Sometimes the phonetics may seem to contradict your pronunciation guide. Don't panic! The easiest and best possible phonetics have been chosen for each individual word. Pronounce the phonetics just as you see them. Don't over-analyze them. Speak with a German accent and, above all, enjoy yourself!

4

When you arrive in **Deutschland** *(doych-lahnt)* Germany or another German-speaking country, the very first thing you will need to do is ask questions — "Where *(voh)* **wo** where is the bus stop?" "**Wo** *(voh)* where can I exchange money?" "**Wo** *(voh)* is the lavatory?" "**Wo** is a restaurant?" "**Wo** do I catch a taxi?" "**Wo** is a good hotel?" "**Wo** is my luggage?" — and the list will go on and on for the entire length of your visit. In German, there are EIGHT KEY QUESTION WORDS to learn. For example, the eight key question words will help you find out exactly what you are ordering in a restaurant before you order it — and not after the surprise (or shock!) arrives. These eight key question words all begin with "**w**" which is pronounced like "v." Take a few minutes to study and practice saying the eight key question words listed below. Then cover the German with your hand and fill in each of the blanks with the matching German **Wort.** *(vort)* word

(voh)
WO = WHERE   *WO, WO, WO, WO, WO*

(vahs)
WAS = WHAT _____

(vair)
WER = WHO _____

(vah-room)
WARUM = WHY _____

(vahn)
WANN = WHEN _____

(vee)
WIE = HOW _____

(vee) *(feel)*
WIE VIEL = HOW MUCH _____

(vee) *(fee-luh)*
WIE VIELE = HOW MANY _____

Now test yourself to see if you really can keep these **Wörter** ^(vur-tair) straight in your mind. Draw lines
between the German **und** ^(oont) English equivalents below.

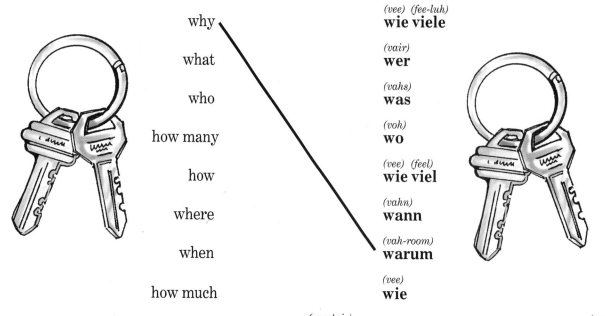

why   (vee) (fee-luh) **wie viele**

what   (vair) **wer**

who   (vahs) **was**

how many   (voh) **wo**

how   (vee) (feel) **wie viel**

where   (vahn) **wann**

when   (vah-room) **warum**

how much   (vee) **wie**

Examine the following questions containing these **Wörter** ^(vur-tair). Practice the sentences out loud **und** ^(oont)
then practice by copying the German in the blanks underneath each question.

(vahs) (ist) (lohs)
Was ist los?
What   is   wrong

_____

(vee) (dair) (zah-laht)
Wie ist der Salat?
How   is   the   salad

_____

(vair) (dahs)
Wer ist das?
Who   is   that

Wer ist das?

(vahn) (kohmt) (dair) (tsook)
Wann kommt der Zug?
When   comes   the   train

_____

(vee) (feel) (koh-stet) (dahs)
Wie viel kostet das?
How   much   costs   that

_____

(voh) (dahs) (tah-lay-fohn)
Wo ist das Telefon?
Where   is   the   telephone

_____

"Wo" ^(voh) will be your most used question **Wort** ^(vort). Say each of the following German sentences
aloud. Then write out each sentence without looking at the example. If you don't succeed on
the first try, don't give up. Just practice each sentence until you are able to do it easily.
Remember **"ei"** is pronounced "eye" **und "ie"** is pronounced "ee." A **"g"** at the end of a word is

6   frequently pronounced like a "k."

(voh) (ist) (eye-nuh) (toy-let-tuh)
Wo ist eine Toilette?
Where · a · toilet

(voh) (ein) (tahk-see)
Wo ist ein Taxi?
Where is a taxi

(voh) (ein) (boos)
Wo ist ein Bus?
Where is bus

DAMEN · HERREN

Wo ist ein Taxi?

(voh) (ein) (res-toh-rahnt)
Wo ist ein Restaurant?

(eye-nuh) (bahnk)
Wo ist eine Bank?
a

(ein) (hoh-tel)
Wo ist ein Hotel?

(yah)
Ja, you can see similarities between **Englisch** and **Deutsch** if you look closely. You will be
yes · *(eng-lish)* English · *(doych)* German

(vur-tair)
amazed at the number of **Wörter** which are identical (or almost identical) in both languages.
words

Of course, they do not always sound the same when spoken by a German speaker, but the

(oont)
similarities will certainly surprise you **und** make your work here easier. Listed below are five
and

(vur-tair) *(ah)* *(vort)*
"free" **Wörter** beginning with "**A**" to help you get started. Be sure to say each **Wort** aloud **und**

(vort)
then write out the German **Wort** in the blanks to the right.

☑ **die Adresse** *(ah-dres-suh)*	address	*die Adresse, die Adresse, die Adresse*
❑ **das Afrika** *(ah-frih-kah)*	Africa	
❑ **die Akademie** *(ah-kah-deh-mee)*	academy	**a**
❑ **der Akt** *(ahkt)*	act (of a play)	
❑ **der Akzent** *(ahk-tsent)*	accent	

(vur-tair)
Free **Wörter** like these will appear at the bottom of the following pages in a yellow color band.

They are easy — enjoy them! Remember, in German, the letter "**ß**" is pronounced "ss."

(doych)
Deutsch has multiple **Wörter** *(vur-tair)* for "the" and "a," but they are very easy.
German   words

(dair) **der** the	*(dee)* **die** the	*(dahs)* **das** the	*(dehn)* **den** the	*(dehm)* **dem** the	*(des)* **des** the

(ein) **ein** a	*(eye-nuh)* **eine** a	*(eye-nen)* **einen** a	*(eye-nair)* **einer** a	*(eye-nem)* **einem** a	*(eye-nes)* **eines** a

(mahn)
der Mann
the   man

(frow)
die Frau
the   woman

(kint)
das Kind
the   child

(fah-tair)
den Vater
father

(froy-line)
dem Fräulein
young woman

(ow-tohs)
des Autos
car

(mahn)
ein Mann
a   man

(frow)
eine Frau
a   woman

(kint)
ein Kind
a   child

(fah-tair)
einen Vater
father

(froy-line)
einem Fräulein
young woman

(ow-tohs)
eines Autos

This might appear difficult at first, but only because it is different from **Englisch** *(eng-lish)*. Just remember you will be understood whether you say "**das Kind** *(kint)*" or "**die Kind**." Soon you will automatically select the right **Wort** without even thinking about it.

In Step 2 you were introduced to the Eight Key QuestionWords. These eight words are the basics, the most essential building blocks for learning German. Throughout this book you will come across keys asking you to fill in the missing question word. Use this opportunity not only to fill in the blank on that key, but to review all your question words. Play with the new sounds, speak slowly and have fun.

❏ **der Alkohol** *(ahl-koh-hohl)* . . . . alcohol _____
❏ **alle** *(ahl-luh)* . . . . all _____
❏ **das Amerika** *(ah-mair-ih-kah)* . . . . America _____
❏ **der Amerikaner** *(ah-mair-ih-kahn-air)* . . . . American (male) _____
❏ **der Apfel** *(ahp-fel)* . . . . apple _____

Before you proceed *(mit)* **mit** *with* this Step, situate yourself comfortably in your living room. Now look around you. Can you name the things that you see in this *(tsih-mair)* **Zimmer** *room* in German? You can probably guess **die Lampe** *(dee) (lahm-puh)* *the lamp* and maybe even **das Sofa.** *(dahs) (zoh-fah)* *the sofa* Let's learn the rest of them. After practicing these **Wörter** *(vur-tair)* out loud, write them in the blanks below.

(dee) (lahm-puh)
die Lampe _____
lamp

(dahs) (zoh-fah)
das Sofa _____
sofa

(dair) (shtool)
der Stuhl _____
chair

(tep-eeH)
der Teppich _____
carpet

(tish)
der Tisch *der Tisch, der Tisch*
table

(dee) (tewr)
die Tür _____
door

(oor)
die Uhr _____
clock

(dair) (for-hahng)
der Vorhang _____
curtain

(tay-lay-fohn)
das Telefon _____
telephone

(fehn-stair)
das Fenster
window
_____

(bilt)
das Bild
picture
_____

You will notice that the correct form of **der**, **die**, or **das** *(dair) (dee) (dahs)* is given **mit** *with* each noun. This tells you whether the noun is masculine (**der**), feminine (**die**) or neuter (**das**). Now open your book to the sticky labels on page 17 and later on page 35. Peel off the first 11 labels **und** *(oont)* *and* proceed around the **Zimmer** *(tsih-mair)* *room* labeling these items in your home. This will help to increase your **deutsche Wort** *(doy-chuh) (vort)* *German word* power easily. Don't forget to say each **Wort** as you attach the label.

Now ask yourself, „**Wo ist die Lampe?**" *(dee) (lahm-puh)* **und** point at it while you answer, „**Dort ist die Lampe.**" *(dort)* *there*

Continue on down the list above until you feel comfortable with these new **Wörter.**

❑ **der Appetit** *(ah-peh-teet)*	appetite	_____
❑ **der April** *(ah-pril)*	April	_____
❑ **der August** *(ow-goost)*	August	**a** _____
❑ **das Auto** *(ow-toh)*	car, automobile	_____
❑ **der Autor** *(ow-tor)*	author	_____

(dahs) (house)
das Haus = the house

(dort) *(house)*
Dort ist das Haus.
there   house

(bew-roh)
das Büro
office

(bah-duh-tsih-mair)
das Badezimmer
bathroom

(kew-Huh)
die Küche
kitchen

(shlahf-tsih-mair)
das Schlafzimmer
bedroom

(ess-tsih-mair)
das Esszimmer
dining room

(vohn-tsih-mair)
das Wohnzimmer
living room

(gah-rah-zhuh)
die Garage
garage

(kel-air)
der Keller
basement

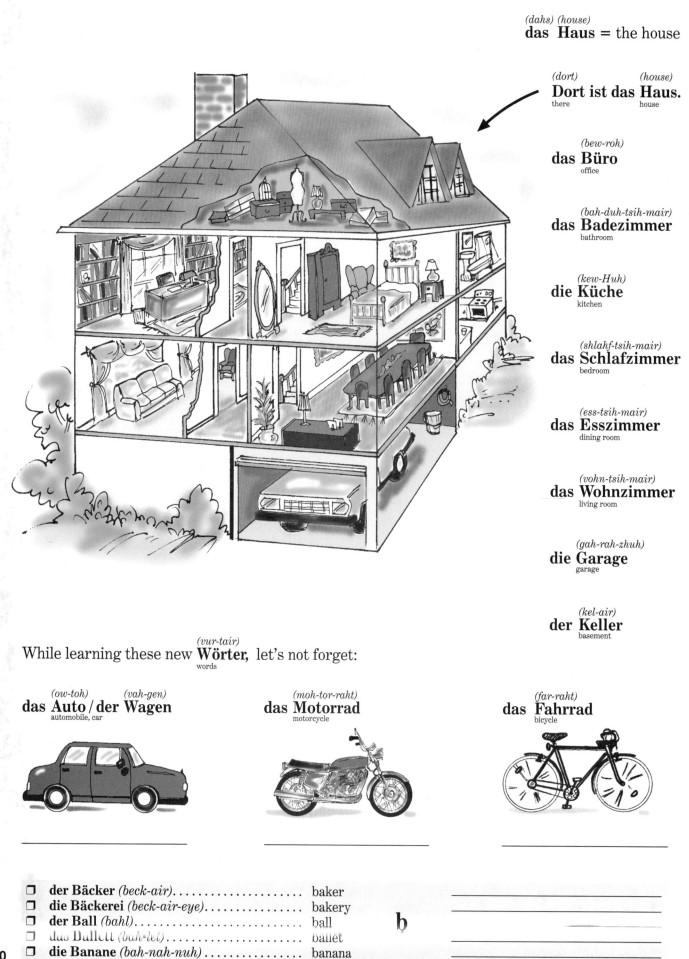

(vur-tair)
While learning these new **Wörter,** let's not forget:
words

(ow-toh) *(vah-gen)*
das Auto / der Wagen
automobile, car

(moh-tor-raht)
das Motorrad
motorcycle

(far-raht)
das Fahrrad
bicycle

❑ **der Bäcker** *(beck-air)*	baker
❑ **die Bäckerei** *(beck-air-eye)*	bakery
❑ **der Ball** *(bahl)*	ball
❑ das Ballett *(bah-let)*	ballet
❑ **die Banane** *(bah-nah-nuh)*	banana

b

(kuh-tsuh)
die Katze
cat

(gar-ten)
der Garten
garden

(bloo-men)
die Blumen
flowers

der Garten, der Garten

(hoont)
der Hund
dog

(breef-kah-sten)
der Briefkasten
mailbox

(post)
die Post
mail

Peel off the next set of labels **und** wander through your **Haus** learning these new **Wörter.** It will
be somewhat difficult to label your **Katze, die Blumen oder** your **Hund,** but be creative.
Practice by asking yourself, „**Wo ist das Auto?**" and reply, „**Dort ist das Auto.**"

(voh) (dahs) (house)
Wo ist das Haus?

☐ **die Bank** *(bahnk)* . . . . bank
☐ **das Beefsteak** *(beef-steak)* . . . . steak
☐ **das Bett** *(bet)* . . . . bed
☐ **besser** *(bes-air)* . . . . better
☐ **das Bier** *(beer)* . . . . beer

b

Consider for a minute how important numbers are. How could you tell someone your phone

number, your address **oder** *(oh-dair)* your hotel room if you had no numbers? And think of how difficult
      or

it would be if you could not understand the time, the price of a **Bier oder** *(beer)* the correct bus to

take. When practicing **die Nummern** *(noo-mairn)* below, notice the similarities which have been underlined
        numbers

for you between **vier und** *(fear)* **vierzehn,** *(fear-tsayn)* **drei** *(dry)* and **dreizehn, und** *(dry-tsayn)* so on.
    four   fourteen   three   thirteen

0	*(nool)* **null**		10	*(tsayn)* **zehn**	
1	*(eins)* **eins**		11	*(elf)* **elf**	
2	*(tsvy)* **zwei**		12	*(ts-vurlf)* **zwölf**	
3	*(dry)* **drei**		13	*(dry-tsayn)* **dreizehn**	
4	*(fear)* **vier**		14	*(fear-tsayn)* **vierzehn**	
5	*(fewnf)* **fünf**		15	*(fewnf-tsayn)* **fünfzehn**	
6	*(zeks)* **sechs**		16	*(zeks-tsayn)* **sechzehn**	
7	*(zee-ben)* **sieben**	*sieben, sieben, sieben*	17	*(zeep-tsayn)* **siebzehn**	
8	*(ahHt)* **acht**		18	*(ahHt-tsayn)* **achtzehn**	
9	*(noyn)* **neun**		19	*(noyn-tsayn)* **neunzehn**	
10	*(tsayn)* **zehn**		20	*(tsvahn-tsig)* **zwanzig**	

☑ **blau** *(blau)* . . . . blue   *blau, blau, blau, blau, blau*
☐ **das Boot** *(boht)* . . . . boat
☐ **braun** *(brown)* . . . . brown   **h**
☐ **bringen** *(bring-en)* . . . . to bring
☐ **die Butter** *(boo-tair)* . . . . butter

Use these **Nummern** *(noo-mairn)* on a daily basis. Count to yourself **auf** *(owf)* **Deutsch** *(doych)* when you brush your teeth, exercise **oder** commute to work. Fill in the blanks below according to the **Nummern** *(noo-mairn)* given in parentheses. Now is also a good time to learn these two very important phrases.

ich möchte *(eeH) (murk-tuh)* _____
I would like

wir möchten *(veer) (murk-ten)* _____
we would like

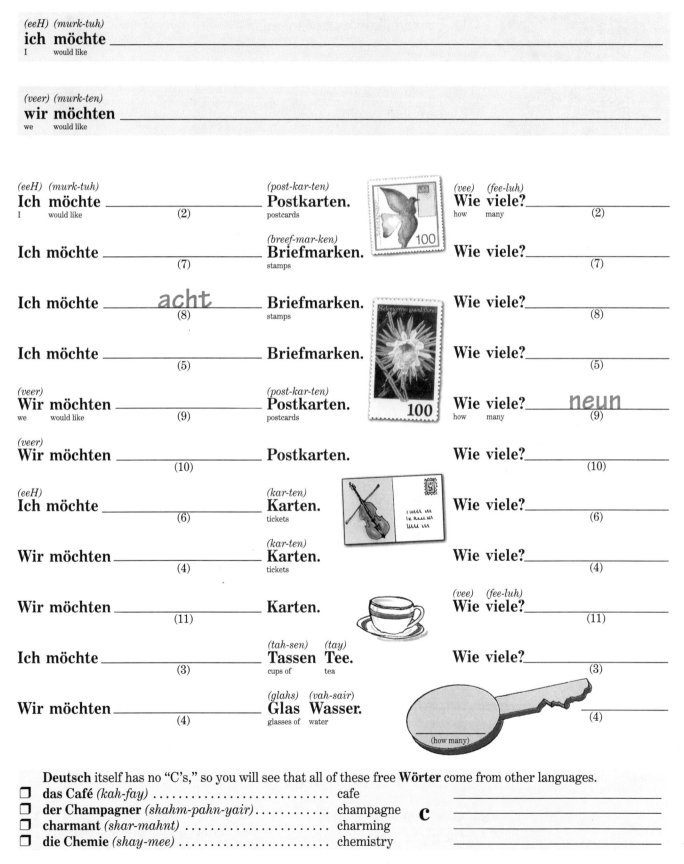

Ich möchte *(eeH) (murk-tuh)* _____ (2) **Postkarten.** *(post-kar-ten)* postcards   **Wie viele?** *(vee) (fee-luh)* _____ (2)
I would like

Ich möchte _____ (7) **Briefmarken.** *(breef-mar-ken)* stamps   **Wie viele?** _____ (7)

Ich möchte _*acht*_ (8) **Briefmarken.** stamps   **Wie viele?** _____ (8)

Ich möchte _____ (5) **Briefmarken.**   **Wie viele?** _____ (5)

Wir möchten *(veer)* _____ (9) **Postkarten.** *(post-kar-ten)* postcards   **Wie viele?** _*neun*_ (9) how many
we would like

Wir möchten *(veer)* _____ (10) **Postkarten.**   **Wie viele?** _____ (10)

Ich möchte *(eeH)* _____ (6) **Karten.** *(kar-ten)* tickets   **Wie viele?** _____ (6)

Wir möchten _____ (4) **Karten.** *(kar-ten)* tickets   **Wie viele?** _____ (4)

Wir möchten _____ (11) **Karten.**   **Wie viele?** *(vee) (fee-luh)* _____ (11)

Ich möchte _____ (3) **Tassen Tee.** *(tah-sen) (tay)* cups of tea   **Wie viele?** _____ (3)

Wir möchten _____ (4) **Glas Wasser.** *(glahs) (vah-sair)* glasses of water   _____ (4) (how many)

Deutsch itself has no "C's," so you will see that all of these free **Wörter** come from other languages.

☐ **das Café** *(kah-fay)* . . . . cafe _____

☐ **der Champagner** *(shahm-pahn-yair)* . . . . champagne **c** _____

☐ **charmant** *(shar-mahnt)* . . . . charming _____

☐ **die Chemie** *(shay-mee)* . . . . chemistry _____

Now see if you can translate the following thoughts into **Deutsch**. *(doych)* German **Die Antworten** *(ahnt-vor-ten)* answers are provided upside down at the bottom of the **Seite**. *(zy-tuh)* page

1. I would like seven postcards.

   _____

2. I would like nine stamps.

   _____

3. We would like four cups of tea.

   _____

4. We would like three tickets.

   _____

Review **die Nummern** *(noo-mairn)* 1 through 20. Write out your telephone number, fax number, **und** *(oont)* cellular number. Then write out a friend's telephone number and a relative's telephone number.

<u>(2</u> <u>0</u> <u>6)</u> <u>2</u> <u>8</u> <u>4</u> — <u>4</u> <u>2</u> <u>1</u> <u>1</u>

zwei null sechs _____

(_____) _____ _____ _____ — _____ _____ _____ _____

_____

(_____) _____ _____ _____ — _____ _____ _____ _____

_____

6   *(dee)* *(far-ben)* **Die Farben**
colors

(far-ben) *(zint)* *(doych-lahnt)*
Die Farben sind the same **in Deutschland** as they are in the United States — they just have
colors   are   in

(nah-meh) *(vee-oh-let)* *(poor-poor)*
different **Namen.** You can easily recognize **violett** as violet and **purpur** as purple. Let's learn
names

(far-ben)
the basic **Farben** so when you are invited to someone's **Haus und** you want to bring flowers, you
house

will be able to order the color you want. Once you've learned **die Farben,** quiz yourself. What

color are your shoes? Your eyes? Your hair? Your house?

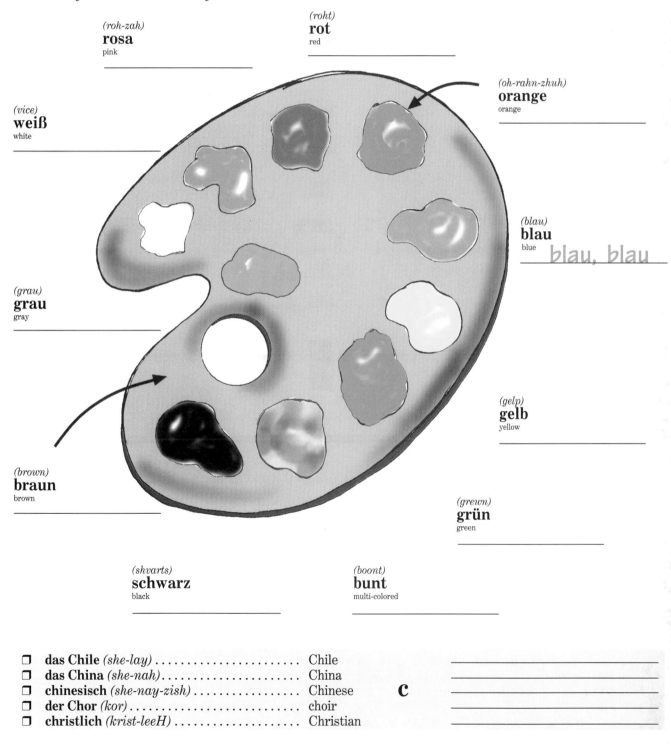

(roh-zah)
rosa
pink

(roht)
rot
red

(oh-rahn-zhuh)
orange
orange

(vice)
weiß
white

(blau)
blau
blue   blau, blau

(grau)
grau
gray

(gelp)
gelb
yellow

(brown)
braun
brown

(grewn)
grün
green

(shvarts)
schwarz
black

(boont)
bunt
multi-colored

❐ **das Chile** *(she-lay)* . . . . Chile _____
❐ **das China** *(she-nah)* . . . . China _____
❐ **chinesisch** *(she-nay-zish)* . . . . Chinese   **c** _____
❐ **der Chor** *(kor)* . . . . choir _____
❐ **christlich** *(krist-leeH)* . . . . Christian _____

Peel off the next group of labels **und** proceed to label these **Farben** in your **Haus.** Identify the

house

two **oder** three dominant colors in the flags below.

or

Germany _____

Switzerland _____

United States _____

Poland _____

Italy _____

The Netherlands _____

United Kingdom _____

Austria _____

Canada _____

France _____

Czech Republic _____

Luxembourg _____

Denmark _____

Belgium _____

You should be able to use your German language skills in some of the above countries as well as

(gelp)

in **Deutschland.** Did you notice that a **"b"** at the end of a word as in „ **gelb** " can be pronounced

as a "p"?

(tahk-see)

_____ _____ **ist das Taxi?**

(where)   (where)

(lohs)

_____ _____ **ist los?**

(what)   (what)   is   wrong

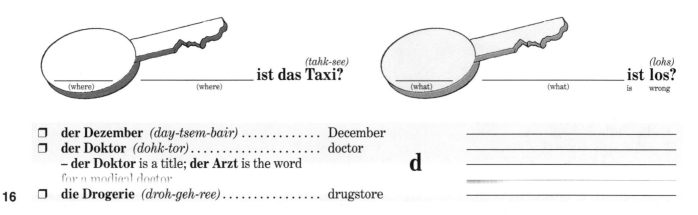

❏ **der Dezember** *(day-tsem-bair)* . . . . December _____
❏ **der Doktor** *(dohk-tor)* . . . . doctor _____
    – **der Doktor** is a title; **der Arzt** is the word   **d**
    for a medical doctor. _____

16   ❏ **die Drogerie** *(droh-geh-ree)* . . . . drugstore

(lahm-puh) **die Lampe**	*(ow-toh)* **das Auto**	*(brown)* **braun**	*(beer)* **das Bier**
(zoh-fah) **das Sofa**	*(moh-tor-raht)* **das Motorrad**	*(roht)* **rot**	*(milsh)* **die Milch**
(shtool) **der Stuhl**	*(far-raht)* **das Fahrrad**	*(roh-zah)* **rosa**	*(boo-tair)* **die Butter**
(tep-eeH) **der Teppich**	*(kah-tsuh)* **die Katze**	*(oh-rahn-zhuh)* **orange**	*(zahlts)* **das Salz**
(tish) **der Tisch**	*(gar-ten)* **der Garten**	*(vice)* **weiß**	*(fef-air)* **der Pfeffer**
(tewr) **die Tür**	*(bloo-men)* **die Blumen**	*(gelp)* **gelb**	*(vine-glahs)* **das Weinglas**
(oor) **die Uhr**	*(hoont)* **der Hund**	*(grau)* **grau**	*(glahs)* **das Glas**
(for-hahng) **der Vorhang**	*(breef-kah-sten)* **der Briefkasten**	*(shvarts)* **schwarz**	*(tsy-toong)* **die Zeitung**
(tay-lay-fohn) **das Telefon**	*(post)* **die Post**	*(blau)* **blau**	*(tah-suh)* **die Tasse**
(fehn-stair) **das Fenster**	*(nool)* **0 null**	*(grewn)* **grün**	*(lur-fel)* **der Löffel**
(bilt) **das Bild**	*(eins)* **1 eins**	*(boont)* **bunt**	*(mes-air)* **das Messer**
(house) **das Haus**	*(tsvy)* **2 zwei**	*(goo-ten) (mor-gen)* **Guten Morgen**	*(zair-vee-et-tuh)* **die Serviette**
(bew-roh) **das Büro**	*(dry)* **3 drei**	*(goo-ten) (tahk)* **Guten Tag**	*(tel-air)* **der Teller**
(bah-duh-tsih-mair) **das Badezimmer**	*(fear)* **4 vier**	*(goo-ten) (ah-bent)* **Guten Abend**	*(gah-bel)* **die Gabel**
(kew-Huh) **die Küche**	*(fewnf)* **5 fünf**	*(goo-tuh) (nahHt)* **Gute Nacht**	*(shrahnk)* **der Schrank**
(shlahf-tsih-mair) **das Schlafzimmer**	*(zeks)* **6 sechs**	*(owf) (vee-dair-zay-en)* **Auf Wiedersehen**	*(tay)* **der Tee**
(ess-tsih-mair) **das Esszimmer**	*(zee-ben)* **7 sieben**	*(vee) (gate) (es) (ee-nen)* **Wie geht es Ihnen?**	*(kah-fay)* **der Kaffee**
(vohn-tsih-mair) **das Wohnzimmer**	*(ahHt)* **8 acht**	*(kewl-shrahnk)* **der Kühlschrank**	*(broht)* **das Brot**
(gah-rah-zhuh) **die Garage**	*(noyn)* **9 neun**	*(oh-fen)* **der Ofen**	*(bit-tuh)* **bitte**
(kel-air) **der Keller**	*(tsayn)* **10 zehn**	*(vine)* **der Wein**	*(dahn-kuh)* **danke**

STICKY LABELS

This book has over 150 special sticky labels for you to use as you learn new words. When you are introduced to one of these words, remove the corresponding label from these pages. Be sure to use each of these unique self-adhesive labels by adhering them to a picture, window, lamp, or whatever object they refer to. And yes, they are removable! The sticky labels make learning to speak German much more fun and a lot easier than you ever expected. For example, when you look in the mirror and see the label, say

(dair) *(shpee-gel)*
„der Spiegel."
mirror

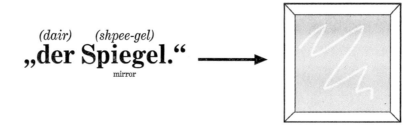

Don't just say it once, say it again and again. And once you label the refrigerator, you should never again open that door without saying

(kewl-shrahnk)
„der Kühlschrank."
refrigerator

By using the sticky labels, you not only learn new words, but friends and family learn along with you! The sooner you start, the sooner you can use these labels at home or work.

7   *(dahs)*   *(gelt)*
Das Geld
money

Before starting this Step, go back and review Step 5. It is important that you can count to

(tsvahn-tsig)
zwanzig without looking at **das Buch.** Let's learn the larger **Nummern** now. After practicing
twenty   *(booH)*   *(noo-mairn)*
book

(dee) (doy-chen)
aloud **die deutschen Nummern** 10 through 1,000 below, write these **Nummern** in the blanks

provided. Again, notice the similarities (underlined) between numbers such as **vier** (4),
(fear)

(fear-tsayn)   *(fear-tsig)*
vierzehn (14), **und** **vierzig** (40).

10	*(tsayn)* **zehn**	_____
20	*(tsvahn-tsig)* **zwanzig**	_____
30	*(dry-sig)* **dreißig**	_____
40	*(fear-tsig)* **vierzig**	*vierzig, vierzig, vierzig, vierzig, vierzig*
50	*(fewnf-tsig)* **fünfzig**	_____
60	*(zek-tsig)* **sechzig**	_____
70	*(zeep-tsig)* **siebzig**	_____
80	*(ahHt-tsig)* **achtzig**	_____
90	*(noyn-tsig)* **neunzig**	_____
100	*(hoon-dairt)* **hundert**	_____
500	*(fewnf-hoon-dairt)* **fünfhundert**	_____
1.000	*(tau-zent)* **tausend**	_____

(tsvy)
Here are **zwei** important phrases to go with all these **Nummern.** Say them out loud over and

over and then write them out twice as many times.

(eeH) *(hah-buh)*
ich habe _____
I   have

(veer) *(hah-ben)*
wir haben _____
we   have

❏   **das Eis** *(ice)* . . . . ice cream   _____
❏   **der Elefant** *(ay-lay-fahnt)* . . . . elephant   _____
❏   **das England** *(eng-lahnt)* . . . . England   **e**   _____
     — where they speak **Englisch** *(eng-lish)*   _____
❏   **das Europa** *(oy-roh-pah)* . . . . Europe

19

The unit of currency **in Deutschland** *(doych-lahnt)* **ist der Euro,** *(oy-roh)* abbreviated "**€**". Let's learn the various kinds of **Geldstücke** *(gelt-shtew-kuh)* **und** **Geldscheine.** *(gelt-shy-nuh)* Always be sure to practice each **Wort** out loud. You might want to exchange some money **jetzt** *(yets-t)* so that you can familiarize yourself **mit** the various types of **Geld.** *(gelt)*

coins — bills — now — with — money

Geldscheine *(gelt-shy-nuh)*
bills

Geldstücke *(gelt-shtew-kuh)*
coins

fünf Euro *(fewnf) (oy-roh)*

fünf Cent *(fewnf) (sent)*

zehn Euro *(tsayn)*

zehn Cent

zwanzig Euro *(tsvahn-tsig)*

zwanzig Cent

fünfzig Cent

fünfzig Euro *(fewnf-tsig)*

ein Euro *(oy-roh)*

hundert Euro *(hoon-dairt)*

zwei Euro *(tsvy)*

❑	**europäisch** *(oy-roh-pay-ish)*	European
❑	**die Familie** *(fah-mee-lee-uh)*	family
❑	**fantastisch** *(fahn-tahs-tish)*	fantastic
	Das ist fantastisch!	That's fantastic!
❑	**der Film** *(film)*	film

e _____

f _____

Review **die Nummern** **zehn** *(tsayn)* through **tausend** *(tau-zent)* again. **Nun,** *(noon)* how do you say "twenty two" **oder** *(oh-dair)*
now

"fifty-three" **auf Deutsch?** *(owf)* *(doych)* You basically talk backwards — "two and twenty" **oder** " *(zwei-und-zwanzig)* three and *(drei-und-*
in   German

fifty". *(fünfzig)* See if you can say **und** write out **die Nummern** on this **Seite.** *(zy-tuh)* The answers **sind** *(zint)* at the
page   are

bottom of the **Seite.**

1. _____   2. ____dreiundachtzig____
   (25 = 5 + 20)   (83 = 3 + 80)

3. _____   4. _____
   (47 = 7 + 40)   (96 = 6 + 90)

Now, how would you say the following **auf Deutsch?** *(owf)* *(doych)*

5. _____
   (I have 80 Euro.)

6. _____
   (We have 72 Euro.)

To ask how much something costs **auf Deutsch,** one asks — „ **Wie viel kostet das?** " *(vee)* *(feel)* *(koh-stet)* *(dahs)*

Now you try it. _____
                (How much does that cost?)

Answer the following questions based on the numbers in parentheses.

7. **Wie viel kostet das? Es kostet** _____ **Euro.** *(oy-roh)*
   (vee) *(feel)* *(koh-stet)* *(dahs)* *(es)* *(koh-stet)*   (10)
   costs that it costs

8. **Wie viel kostet das Bild?** *(bilt)* **Das Bild kostet** _____ **Euro.**
                              picture   (20)

9. **Wie viel kostet das Buch?** *(booH)* **Das Buch kostet** *(booH)* _____ **Euro.**
                              book   (17)

10. **Wie viel kostet der Film?** *(film)* **Der Film kostet** _____ **Euro.**
                                                          (6)

ANTWORTEN

5. Ich habe achtzig Euro.	10. sechs
4. sechsundneunzig	9. siebzehn
3. siebenundvierzig	8. zwanzig
2. dreiundachtzig	7. zehn
1. Fünfundzwanzig	6. Wir haben zweiundsiebzig Euro.

21

Heute, Morgen und Gestern

(hoy-tuh) today   *(mor-gen)* tomorrow   *(oont)* and   *(ges-tairn)* yesterday

(dair) *(kah-len-dair)*
der Kalender
the   calendar

_____

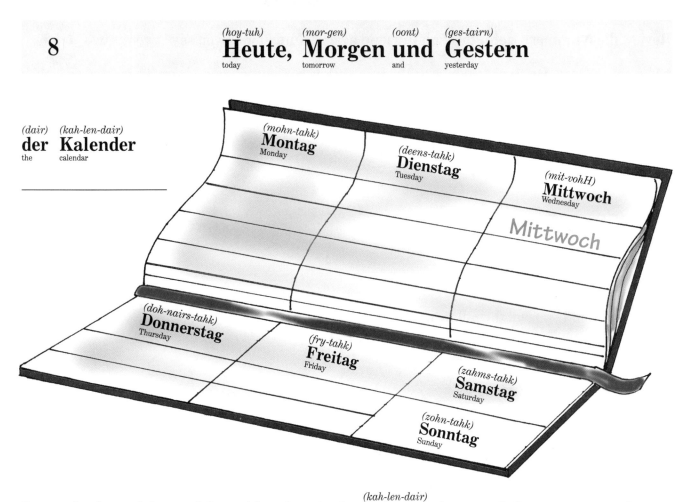

(mohn-tahk) **Montag** Monday

(deens-tahk) **Dienstag** Tuesday

(mit-vohH) **Mittwoch** Wednesday

Mittwoch

(doh-nairs-tahk) **Donnerstag** Thursday

(fry-tahk) **Freitag** Friday

(zahms-tahk) **Samstag** Saturday

(zohn-tahk) **Sonntag** Sunday

Learn the days of the week by writing them in the *(kah-len-dair)* **Kalender** above **und** then move on to the

(fear)
vier parts to each **Tag.**
four   *(tahk)* day

(mor-gen)
der Morgen
morning

(nahH-mit-tahk)
der Nachmittag
afternoon

(ah-bent)
der Abend
evening

(nahHt)
die Nacht
night

_____   _____   _____   _____

❐ **finden** *(fin-den)* .... to find   _____
   — **Ich finde das Hotelzimmer.**
❐ **der Finger** *(fing-air)* .... finger   **f**   _____
❐ der Fisch *(fish)* .... fish   _____
❐ **das Foto** *(foh-toh)* .... photo   _____

Es ist *(zair)* **sehr** important to know the days of the week **und** the various parts of the *(tahk)* **Tag** as well as

(dry) *(vur-tair)*
these **drei Wörter.**
three

(ges-tairn) **gestern**   *(hoy-tuh)* **heute**   *(mor-gen)* **morgen**

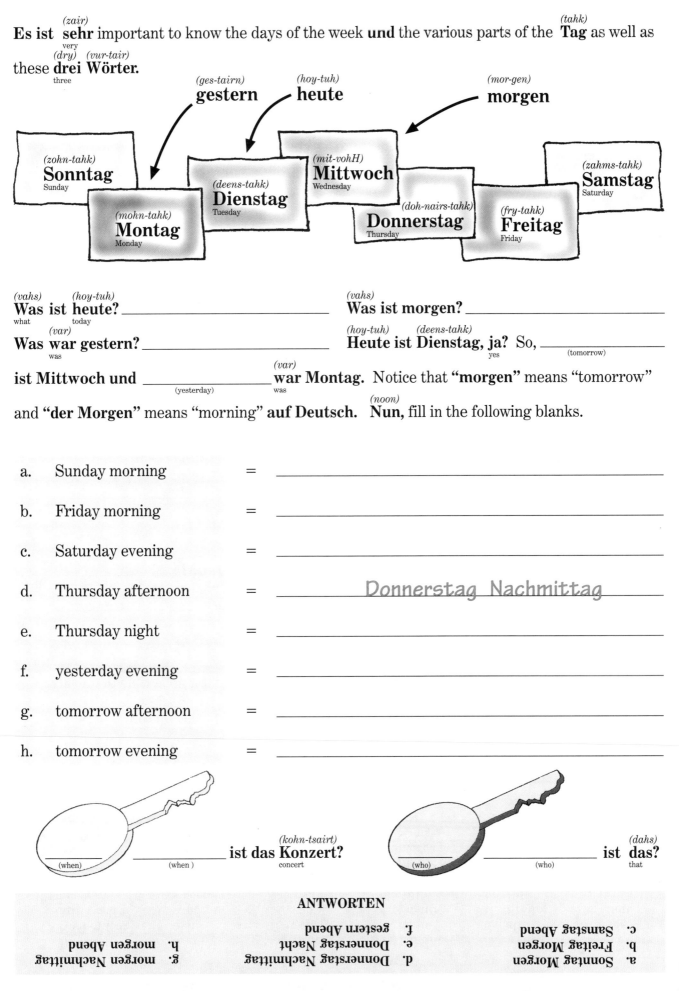

(zohn-tahk) **Sonntag** Sunday

(mohn-tahk) **Montag** Monday

(deens-tahk) **Dienstag** Tuesday

(mit-vohH) **Mittwoch** Wednesday

(doh-nairs-tahk) **Donnerstag** Thursday

(fry-tahk) **Freitag** Friday

(zahms-tahk) **Samstag** Saturday

(vahs) *(hoy-tuh)*
Was ist heute? _____
what   today

(var)
Was war gestern? _____
was

(vahs)
Was ist morgen? _____

(hoy-tuh) *(deens-tahk)*
Heute ist Dienstag, ja? So, _____
yes   (tomorrow)

(var)
ist Mittwoch und _____ **war Montag.** Notice that **"morgen"** means "tomorrow"
                        (yesterday)   was

and **"der Morgen"** means "morning" **auf Deutsch.** *(noon)* **Nun,** fill in the following blanks.

a.   Sunday morning   =   _____

b.   Friday morning   =   _____

c.   Saturday evening   =   _____

d.   Thursday afternoon   =   _____Donnerstag Nachmittag_____

e.   Thursday night   =   _____

f.   yesterday evening   =   _____

g.   tomorrow afternoon   =   _____

h.   tomorrow evening   =   _____

(kohn-tsairt)
___(when)___ ___(when)___ **ist das Konzert?**
concert

(dahs)
___(who)___ ___(who)___ **ist das?**
that

ANTWORTEN

a. **Sonntag Morgen**	c. **Samstag Abend**	
b. **Freitag Morgen**		
d. **Donnerstag Nachmittag**	f. **gestern Abend**	
e. **Donnerstag Nacht**	h. **morgen Abend**	
g. **morgen Nachmittag**		

23

Knowing the parts of the **Tag** *(tahk)* [day] will help you to learn the various **deutsche** *(doy-chuh)* greetings below.

Practice these every day until your trip.

Guten Morgen *(goo-ten) (mor-gen)* [good morning] _____

Guten Tag *(goo-ten) (tahk)* [good day / hello] _____

Guten Abend *(ah-bent)* [good evening] _____

Gute Nacht *(goo-tuh) (nahHt)* [good night] _____

Auf Wiedersehen *(owf) (vee-dair-zay-en)* [good-bye] _____

Take the next **vier** *(fear)* [four] labels **und** stick them on the appropriate **Dinge** *(ding-uh)* [things] in your **Haus** *(house)* [house]. Make sure you attach them to the correct items, as they are only **auf Deutsch** *(owf)*. How about the bathroom mirror **für** *(fewr)* [for] „**Guten Morgen**" *(goo-ten)*? **Oder** *(oh-dair)* [or] your alarm clock **für** *(fewr)* „**Gute Nacht**" *(goo-tuh) (nahHt)*? Let's not forget,

Wie geht es Ihnen? *(vee) (gate) (ee-nen)* [how are you] _____

Now for some „**ja**" *(yah)* [yes] or „**nein**" *(nine)* [no] questions –

Are your eyes **blau**? _____   Are your shoes **braun**? *(brown)* _____

Is your favorite color **rot**? *(roht)* _____   Is today **Samstag**? _____

Do you own a **Katze**? *(kah-tsuh)* _____   Do you own a **Hund**? *(hoont)* _____

You **sind** *(zint)* [are] about one-fourth of your way through this **Buch** *(booH)* [book] **und es ist** *(oont)* [it is] a good time to quickly review **die Wörter** *(vur-tair)* you **haben** *(hah-ben)* [have] learned before doing the crossword puzzle on the next **Seite** *(zy-tuh)* [page].

Viel Spaß und viel Glück! *(feel) (shpahs) (feel) (glewk)* [have fun much luck]

ANTWORTEN TO THE CROSSWORD PUZZLE

DOWN			ACROSS		
43. wo	28. rot	14. wer	46. Bier	34. sechzig	20. Bank
42. grün	25. Bild	13. Samstag	45. Büro	32. der / die / das	19. Abend
40. Zug	24. bunt	11. morgen	44. gut	31. Deutsch	18. fünf
38. vierzig	23. eins	8. Montag	43. warum	29. gestern	17. frei
37. grau	21. kommen	6. Nacht	41. Tag	28. rosa	15. wie viel
36. Bett	20. Bus	5. Auto	39. zwanzig	27. sieben	12. Donnerstag
33. Tee	17. Freitag	4. Sonntag	38. vier	26. Amerika	10. heute
30. schwarz	16. elf	2. neun	37. gelb	24. blau	9. Mittwoch
	15. weiß	1. Familie			7. Nachmittag
					3. Dienstag

24

CROSSWORD PUZZLE (DAS KREUZWORTRÄTSEL)

(kroits-vort-rate-zel)

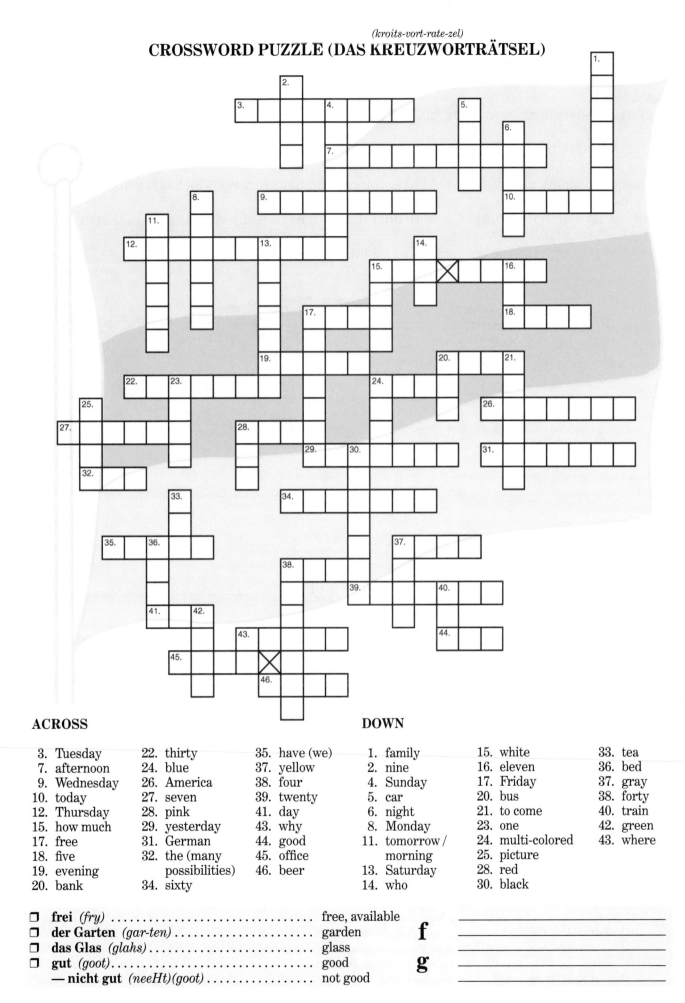

ACROSS

3. Tuesday
7. afternoon
9. Wednesday
10. today
12. Thursday
15. how much
17. free
18. five
19. evening
20. bank

22. thirty
24. blue
26. America
27. seven
28. pink
29. yesterday
31. German
32. the (many possibilities)
34. sixty

35. have (we)
37. yellow
38. four
39. twenty
41. day
43. why
44. good
45. office
46. beer

DOWN

1. family
2. nine
4. Sunday
5. car
6. night
8. Monday
11. tomorrow / morning
13. Saturday
14. who

15. white
16. eleven
17. Friday
20. bus
21. to come
23. one
24. multi-colored
25. picture
28. red
30. black

33. tea
36. bed
37. gray
38. forty
40. train
42. green
43. where

❑ **frei** *(fry)* . . . . free, available
❑ **der Garten** *(gar-ten)* . . . . garden **f** _____
❑ **das Glas** *(glahs)* . . . . glass _____
❑ **gut** *(goot)* . . . . good **g** _____
— **nicht gut** *(neeHt)(goot)* . . . . not good _____

25

(in) *(ahn)* *(owf)*
In, an, auf...
in   on   on top of

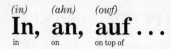

(doy-chuh)
Deutsche prepositions (words like "in," "on," "through" and "next to") **sind** easy to learn **und**
(zint) (oont)
are

(mit) *(zeks)*
they allow you to be precise **mit** a minimum of effort. Instead of having to point **sechs** times
with

at a piece of yummy pastry you would like, you can explain precisely which one you want by

(oh-dair)
saying **es ist** behind, in front of, next to **oder** under the piece of pastry that the salesperson is
it is

(vur-tair)
starting to pick up. Let's learn some of these little **Wörter.**

(oon-tair)
unter_____
under

(ew-bair)
über_____
over

(owf)
auf _____
on top of (horizontal surfaces)

(nay-ben)
neben _____
next to

(ahn)
an _____
on / upon (vertical surfaces) / at the edge of

(in)
in _____
into / in

(for)
vor_____
in front of

(hin-tair)
hinter_____
behind

(ows)
aus _____
out of / from

(tsvih-shen)
zwischen _____
between

(zy-tuh)
Fill in the blanks on the next **Seite** with the correct prepositions from those you **haben** just
(hah-ben)

learned.

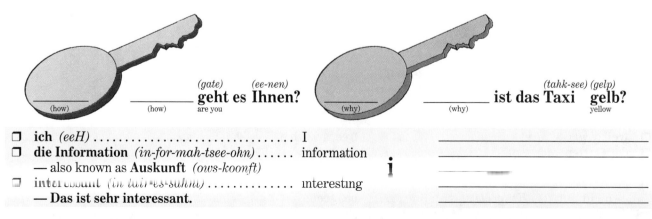

(gate) (ee-nen)
_____ **geht es Ihnen?**
(how)   (how)   are you

_____ **ist das Taxi gelb?**
(why)   (why)   *(tahk-see) (gelp)* yellow

❏ **ich** *(eeH)* I
❏ **die Information** *(in-for-mah-tsee-ohn)* ...... information
   — also known as **Auskunft** *(ows-koonft)*
❏ **interessant** *(in-tair-es-sahnt)* .... interesting
   — **Das ist sehr interessant.**

i

_____

_____

_____

Der Kuchen ist _(koo-Hen)_ _____ **dem Tisch.** _(dehm) (tish)_
pastry / cake   (on)   table

Der Hund ist _(hoont)_ _____ **dem Tisch.**
dog   (under)   table

Der Arzt ist _(arts-t)_ _____ **dem guten Hotel.** _(goo-ten)_
doctor   (in)   good

Wo ist der Arzt? _(voh) (arts-t)_ _____

Der Mann ist _(mahn)_ _____ **dem Hotel.**
man   (in front of)

Wo ist der Mann? _(mahn)_ _____

Das Telefon ist _(tay-lay-fohn)_ _____ **dem Bild.** _(bilt)_
telephone   (next to)   picture

Wo ist das Telefon? _(voh) (dahs) (tay-lay-fohn)_ _____

Nun, _(noon)_ fill in each blank on the picture below with the best possible one of these little **Wörter.**
now

Do you recognize **das Heidelberger** _(hi-del-bair-gair)_ **Schloss** _(shlohss)_ below?
Heidelberg   castle

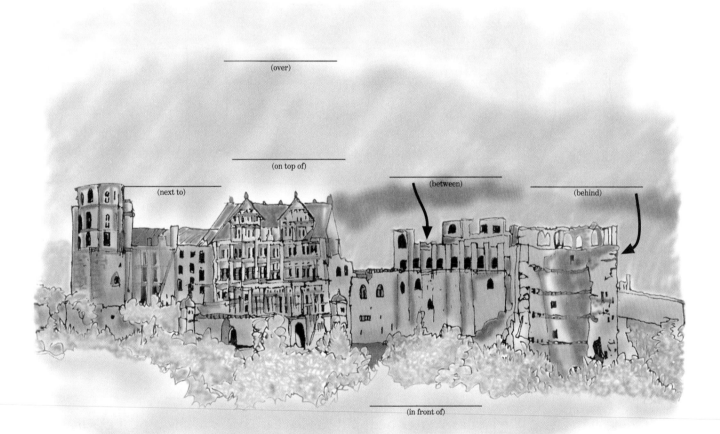

_____
(over)

_____
(on top of)

_____
(next to)

_____
(between)

_____
(behind)

_____
(in front of)

_____
(under)

❏ **das Institut** _(in-stee-toot)_ .... institution
❏ **das Italien** _(ee-tah-lee-en)_ .... Italy
  — where they speak **Italienisch** _(ee-tah-lee-ay-nish)_
❏ **ja** _(yah)_ .... yes
❏ **die Jacke** _(yah-kuh)_ .... jacket

i _____

j _____

(yah-noo-ar) *(fay-broo-ar)* *(mairts)*

Januar, Februar, März
January February March

You **haben** *(hah-ben)* learned the days of the **Woche,** *(voh-Huh)* so now **es ist** time to learn **die Monate** *(moh-nah-tuh)* of the **Jahr** *(yar)*
week it is months year

und *(oont)* all the different kinds of **Wetter.** *(vet-tair)*
weather

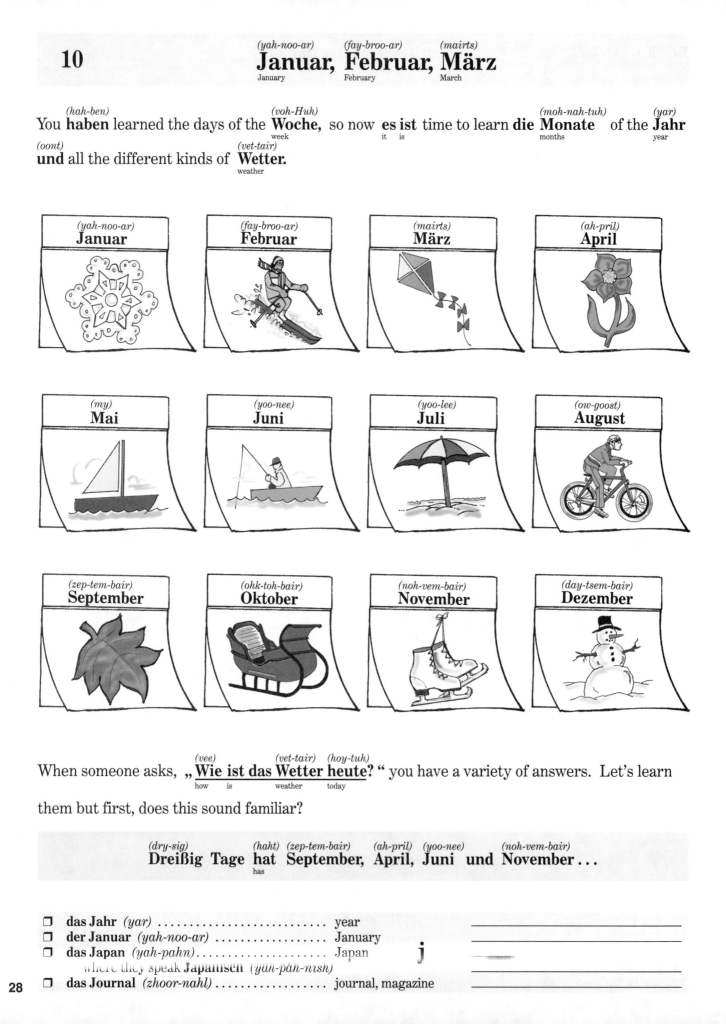

(yah-noo-ar) **Januar**	*(fay-broo-ar)* **Februar**	*(mairts)* **März**	*(ah-pril)* **April**

(my) **Mai**	*(yoo-nee)* **Juni**	*(yoo-lee)* **Juli**	*(ow-goost)* **August**

(zep-tem-bair) **September**	*(ohk-toh-bair)* **Oktober**	*(noh-vem-bair)* **November**	*(day-tsem-bair)* **Dezember**

When someone asks, „ **Wie ist das Wetter heute?** " you have a variety of answers. Let's learn
(vee) *(vet-tair)* *(hoy-tuh)*
how is weather today

them but first, does this sound familiar?

Dreißig Tage hat September, April, Juni und November . . .
(dry-sig) *(haht)* *(zep-tem-bair)* *(ah-pril)* *(yoo-nee)* *(noh-vem-bair)*
has

❏ **das Jahr** *(yar)* . . . . year _____
❏ **der Januar** *(yah-noo-ar)* . . . . January _____
❏ **das Japan** *(yah-pahn)* . . . . Japan **j** _____
where they speak **Japanisch** *(yah-pah-nish)*
❏ **das Journal** *(zhoor-nahl)* . . . . journal, magazine _____

(vee) *(vet-tair)* *(hoy-tuh)*
Wie ist das Wetter heute? _____
today

(shnight) *(yah-noo-ar)*
Es schneit im Januar. _____
it snows in

(owH) *(fay-broo-ar)*
Es schneit auch im Februar. _____
also

(rayg-net) *(mairts)*
Es regnet im März. _____
it rains

(ah-pril)
Es regnet auch im April. _____

(vin-dig) *(my)*
Es ist windig im Mai. _____
windy

(varm) *(yoo-nee)*
Es ist warm im Juni. _____
warm

(shurn) *(yoo-lee)*
Es ist schön im Juli. _____
pretty

(hice) *(ow-goost)*
Es ist heiß im August. _____
hot

(nay-blig) *(zep-tem-bair)*
Es ist neblig im September. _____
foggy

(kewl) *(ohk-toh-bair)*
Es ist kühl im Oktober. _____
cool

(schlehHt) *(noh-vem-bair)*
Es ist schlecht im November. _____
bad

(kahlt) *(day-tsem-bair)*
Es ist kalt im Dezember. _____
cold

(vee) *(vet-tair)*
Wie ist das Wetter im Februar? _____
how

Wie ist das Wetter im April? ___ Es regnet im April. Es regnet im April. ___

Wie ist das Wetter im Mai? _____

Wie ist das Wetter im August? _____

❏ **der Juli** *(yoo-lee)* . . . . July
❏ **der Juni** *(yoo-nee)* . . . . June
   Notice how often **Englisch** "c" becomes "k" **auf Deutsch.**
❏ **der Kaffee** *(kah-fay)* . . . . coffee
❏ **das Kaffeehaus** *(kay-fay-house)* . . . . coffee house

j _____

k _____
_____
_____

Nun für *(fewr)* the seasons of the **Jahr** *(yar)*...
year

der Winter *(vin-tair)*
winter

der Sommer *(zoh-mair)*
summer

der Herbst *(hairp-st)*
autumn

der Frühling *(frew-ling)*
spring

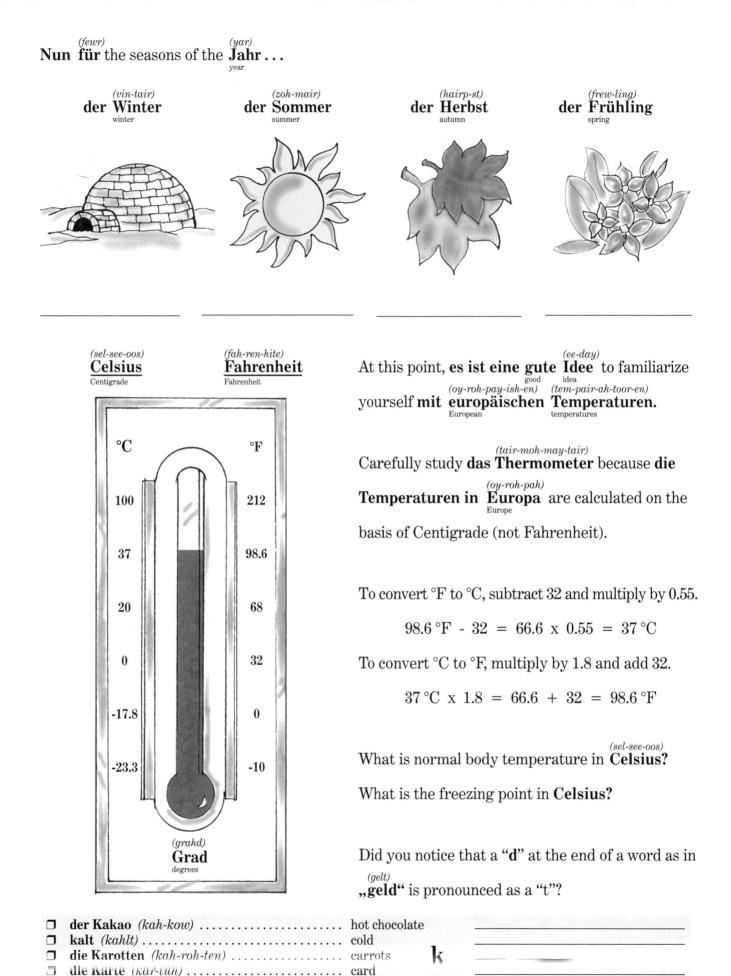

Celsius *(sel-see-oos)*
Centigrade

Fahrenheit *(fah-ren-hite)*
Fahrenheit

°C	°F
100	212
37	98.6
20	68
0	32
-17.8	0
-23.3	-10

Grad *(grahd)*
degrees

At this point, **es ist eine gute Idee** *(ee-day)* to familiarize
good   idea
yourself **mit europäischen** *(oy-roh-pay-ish-en)* **Temperaturen.** *(tem-pair-ah-toor-en)*
European   temperatures

Carefully study **das Thermometer** *(tair-moh-may-tair)* because **die**

Temperaturen in Europa *(oy-roh-pah)* are calculated on the
Europe

basis of Centigrade (not Fahrenheit).

To convert °F to °C, subtract 32 and multiply by 0.55.

$$98.6\,°F - 32 = 66.6 \times 0.55 = 37\,°C$$

To convert °C to °F, multiply by 1.8 and add 32.

$$37\,°C \times 1.8 = 66.6 + 32 = 98.6\,°F$$

What is normal body temperature in **Celsius?** *(sel-see-oos)*

What is the freezing point in **Celsius?**

Did you notice that a "**d**" at the end of a word as in

„**geld**" *(gelt)* is pronounced as a "t"?

❏	**der Kakao** *(kah-kow)*	hot chocolate	_____
❏	**kalt** *(kahlt)*	cold	_____
❏	**die Karotten** *(kah-roh-ten)*	carrots	_____
❏	**die Karte** *(kar-tuh)*	card	_____
❏	**kommen** *(koh-men)*	to come	_____

k

11

(kin-dair) (kew-Huh) (kir-Huh)
Kinder, Küche, und Kirche
children   kitchen   church

Just as we have the three "R's" **auf Englisch, auf Deutsch** there are the three "K's" which help

us to understand some of the basics of German life. Study the family tree below.

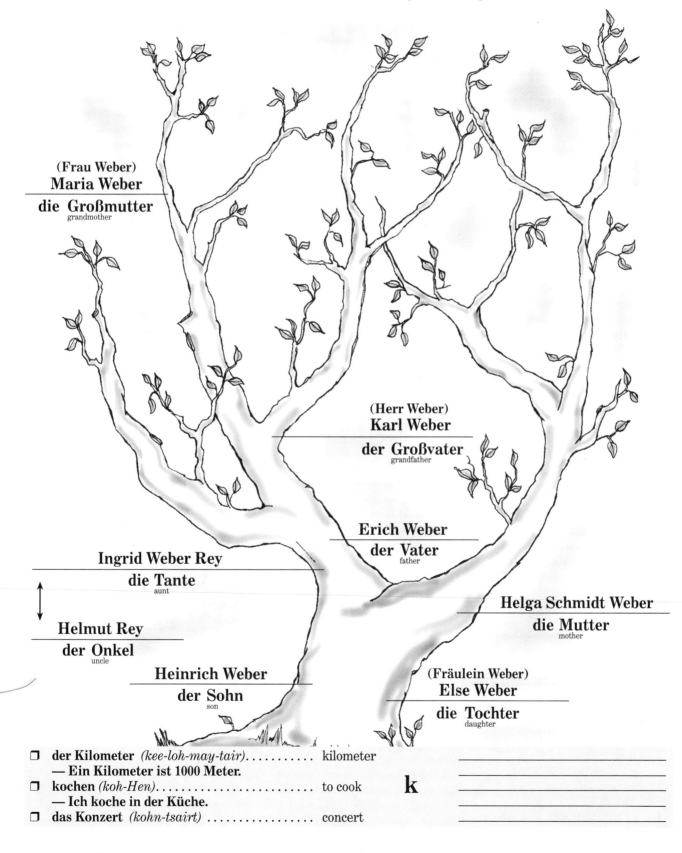

(Frau Weber)
Maria Weber

die Großmutter
grandmother

(Herr Weber)
Karl Weber

der Großvater
grandfather

Erich Weber
der Vater
father

Ingrid Weber Rey
die Tante
aunt

Helga Schmidt Weber
die Mutter
mother

Helmut Rey
der Onkel
uncle

Heinrich Weber
der Sohn
son

(Fräulein Weber)
Else Weber
die Tochter
daughter

❏ **der Kilometer** *(kee-loh-may-tair)*.......... kilometer
— **Ein Kilometer ist 1000 Meter.**
❏ **kochen** *(koh-Hen)*...................... to cook   **k**
— **Ich koche in der Küche.**
❏ **das Konzert** *(kohn-tsairt)* .... concert

Let's learn how to identify **die Familie** *(fah-mee-lee-uh)* by **Name** *(nah-muh)*. Study the following examples carefully.

family   *name*

(vee) (hi-sen) (zee)
Wie heißen Sie? _____
what is your name / how are you called

(eeH) (hi-suh)
Ich heiße _____
my name is / I am called   (your name)

(el-tairn)
die Eltern
parents

(fah-tair)
der Vater _____
father

(vee) (heist) (fah-tair)
Wie heißt der Vater? _____
how   is called   father

(moo-tair)
die Mutter _____
mother

(dee) (moo-tair)
Wie heißt die Mutter? _____
how   mother

(kin-dair)
die Kinder
children

(zohn) *(tohH-tair)*
Der Sohn und die Tochter sind

(broo-dair) *(shves-tair)*
auch Bruder und Schwester!
brother   sister

(zohn)
der Sohn _____
son

(vee) (dair)
Wie heißt der Sohn? _____
son

(tohH-tair)
die Tochter _____
daughter

(heist) (tohH-tair)
Wie heißt die Tochter? _____
daughter

(fair-vahn-ten)
die Verwandten
relatives

(grohs-fah-tair)
der Großvater _____
grandfather

(dair) (grohs-fah-tair)
Wie heißt der Großvater? _____
grandfather

(grohs-moo-tair)
die Großmutter _____
grandmother

(heist)
Wie heißt die Großmutter? _____
grandmother

Now you ask —

_____
(How are you called? / What is your name?)

And answer —

_____
(My name is . . .)

❐ **kosten** *(koh-sten)*	to cost	_____
— **Es kostet 20 Euro.**		
❐ **das Kotelett** *(koh-teh-let)*	cutlet	_____
❐ **kühl** *(kewl)*	cool	_____
❐ **der Kühlschrank** *(kewl-shrahnk)*	refrigerator	

k

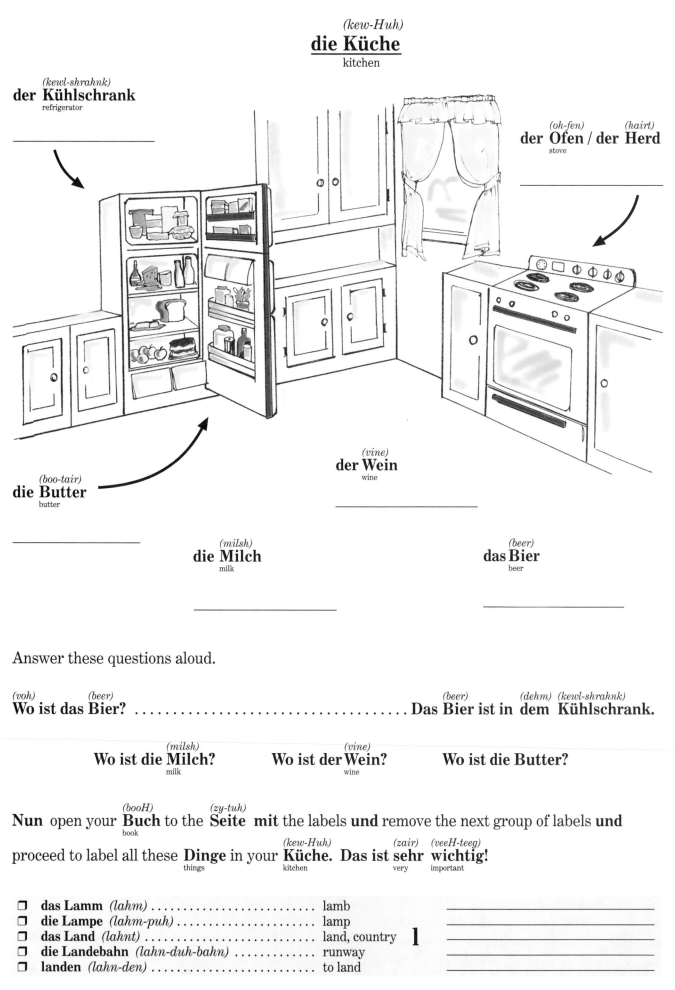

(kew-Huh)
die Küche
kitchen

(kewl-shrahnk)
der Kühlschrank
refrigerator

———————————

(oh-fen) *(hairt)*
der Ofen / der Herd
stove

———————————

(boo-tair)
die Butter
butter

———————————

(vine)
der Wein
wine

———————————

(milsh)
die Milch
milk

———————————

(beer)
das Bier
beer

———————————

Answer these questions aloud.

(voh)   *(beer)*   *(beer)*   *(dehm)*   *(kewl-shrahnk)*
Wo ist das Bier? . . . . **Das Bier ist in dem Kühlschrank.**

(milsh)   *(vine)*
Wo ist die Milch?   **Wo ist der Wein?**   **Wo ist die Butter?**
milk   wine

(booH)   *(zy-tuh)*
Nun open your **Buch** to the **Seite mit** the labels **und** remove the next group of labels **und**
                book

                                 (kew-Huh)   *(zair)*   *(veeH-teeg)*
proceed to label all these **Dinge** in your **Küche. Das ist sehr wichtig!**
                            things   kitchen   very   important

- ❏ **das Lamm** *(lahm)* . . . . lamb   ———————————
- ❏ **die Lampe** *(lahm-puh)* . . . . lamp   ———————————
- ❏ **das Land** *(lahnt)* . . . . land, country   **l** ———————————
- ❏ **die Landebahn** *(lahn-duh-bahn)* . . . . runway   ———————————
- ❏ **landen** *(lahn-den)* . . . . to land   ———————————

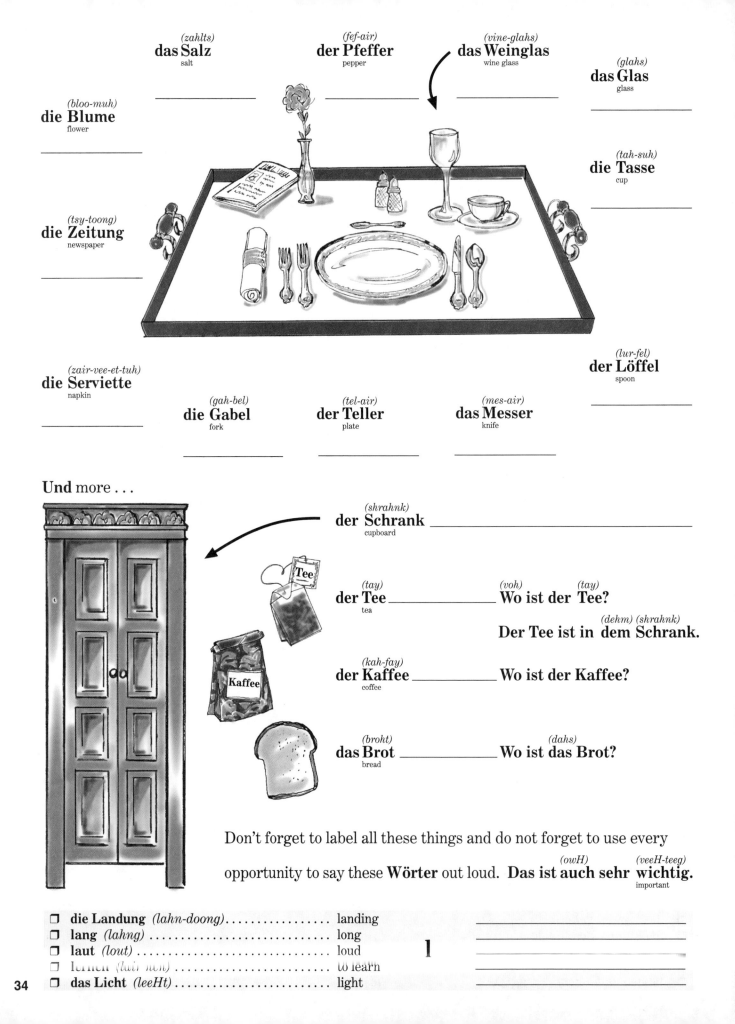

(zahlts)
das Salz
salt

(fef-air)
der Pfeffer
pepper

(vine-glahs)
das Weinglas
wine glass

(glahs)
das Glas
glass

(bloo-muh)
die Blume
flower

(tah-suh)
die Tasse
cup

(tsy-toong)
die Zeitung
newspaper

(zair-vee-et-tuh)
die Serviette
napkin

(lur-fel)
der Löffel
spoon

(gah-bel)
die Gabel
fork

(tel-air)
der Teller
plate

(mes-air)
das Messer
knife

Und more . . .

(shrahnk)
der Schrank _____
cupboard

(tay)
der Tee _____
tea

(voh) *(tay)*
Wo ist der Tee?

(dehm) *(shrahnk)*
Der Tee ist in dem Schrank.

(kah-fay)
der Kaffee _____
coffee

Wo ist der Kaffee?

(broht)
das Brot _____
bread

(dahs)
Wo ist das Brot?

Don't forget to label all these things and do not forget to use every

(owH) *(veeH-teeg)*
opportunity to say these **Wörter** out loud. **Das ist auch sehr wichtig.**
important

❑ **die Landung** *(lahn-doong)* . . . . landing _____
❑ **lang** *(lahng)* . . . . long _____
❑ **laut** *(lout)* . . . . loud _____
❑ **lernen** *(lair-nen)* . . . . to learn _____
❑ **das Licht** *(leeHt)* . . . . light _____

l

34

(ent-shool-dee-goong)
Entschuldigung

(breef)
der Brief

(day-oh)
das Deo

(shorts)
die Shorts

(kly-dair-shrahnk)
der Kleiderschrank

(breef-mar-kuh)
die Briefmarke

(kahm)
der Kamm

(tee-shirt)
das T-shirt

(bet)
das Bett

(post-kar-tuh)
die Postkarte

(ray-gen-mahn-tel)
der Regenmantel

(oon-tair-hoh-zuh)
die Unterhose

(kohpf-kiss-en)
das Kopfkissen

(pahss)
der Pass

(ray-gen-shirm)
der Regenschirm

(oon-tair-hemt)
das Unterhemd

(bet-deck-uh)
die Bettdecke

(kar-tuh)
die Karte

(mahn-tel)
der Mantel

(klite)
das Kleid

(veck-air)
der Wecker

(koh-fair)
der Koffer

(hahnt-shoo-uh)
die Handschuhe

(bloo-zuh)
die Bluse

(shpee-gel)
der Spiegel

(hahnt-tah-shuh)
die Handtasche

(hoot)
der Hut

(rohk)
der Rock

(vahsh-beck-en)
das Waschbecken

(breef-tah-shuh)
die Brieftasche

(shtee-fel)
die Stiefel

(poo-lee)
der Pulli

(tooH)
das Tuch

(gelt)
das Geld

(shoo-uh)
die Schuhe

(oon-tair-rohk)
der Unterrock

(toy-let-tuh)
die Toilette

(kray-deet-kar-ten)
die Kreditkarten

(ten-is-shoo-uh)
die Tennisschuhe

(bay-hah)
der BH

(doosh-uh)
die Dusche

(ry-zuh-shecks)
die Reiseschecks

(ahn-tsook)
der Anzug

(oon-tair-hoh-zuh)
die Unterhose

(bly-shtift)
der Bleistift

(kah-mair-ah)
die Kamera

(krah-vah-tuh)
die Krawatte

(zoh-ken)
die Socken

(fairn-zay-air)
der Fernseher

(bah-tair-ee-en)
die Batterien

(hemt)
das Hemd

(shtroomf-hoh-zuh)
die Strumpfhose

(koo-lee)
der Kuli

(bah-duh-ahn-tsook)
der Badeanzug

(tah-shen-tooH)
das Taschentuch

(shlahf-ahn-tsook)
der Schlafanzug

(booH)
das Buch

(zahn-dah-len)
die Sandalen

(yah-kuh)
die Jacke

(nahHt-hemt)
das Nachthemd

(kohm-pyoo-tair)
der Computer

(zoh-nen-bril-luh)
die Sonnenbrille

(hoh-zuh)
die Hose

(bah-duh-mahn-tel)
der Bademantel

(bril-luh)
die Brille

(tsahn-bewr-stuh)
die Zahnbürste

(jeans)
die Jeans

(house-shoo-uh)
die Hausschuhe

(pah-peer)
das Papier

(tsahn-pah-stah)
die Zahnpasta

(eeH) *(koh-muh)* *(ows)*
Ich komme aus _____.

(pah-peer-korp)
der Papierkorb

(zy-fuh)
die Seife

(eeH) *(murk-tuh)* *(doych)* *(lair-nen)*
Ich möchte Deutsch lernen.

(tsight-shrift)
die Zeitschrift

(rah-zeer-mes-air)
das Rasiermesser

(eeH) *(hi-suh)*
Ich heiße _____.

PLUS...

This book includes a number of other innovative features unique to the *"10 minutes a day*®*"* series. At the back of this book, you will find twelve pages of flash cards. Cut them out and flip through them at least once a day.

On pages 116, 117 and 118 you will find a beverage guide and a menu guide. Don't wait until your trip to use them. Clip out the menu guide and use it tonight at the dinner table. Take them both with you the next time you dine at your favorite German restaurant.

By using the special features in this book, you will be speaking German before you know it.

(feel)   *(shpahs)*
Viel Spaß!
have fun

(kir-Huh)
<u>die Kirche</u>
church

In Deutschland there is not the wide variety of (ray-lee-gee-ohn-en) **Religionen** that (veer) (fin-den) (here) **wir finden hier in** (we) (find)

(ah-mair-ih-kah)
Amerika. A person is usually one of the following.

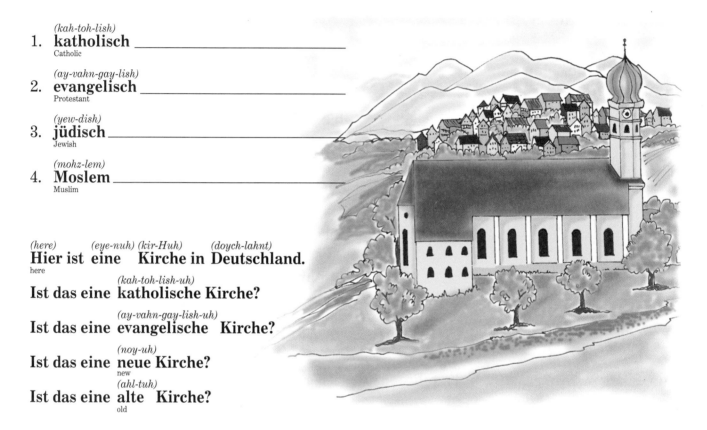

(kah-toh-lish)
1. **katholisch** _____
Catholic

(ay-vahn-gay-lish)
2. **evangelisch** _____
Protestant

(yew-dish)
3. **jüdisch** _____
Jewish

(mohz-lem)
4. **Moslem** _____
Muslim

(here) (eye-nuh) (kir-Huh) (doych-lahnt)
Hier ist eine Kirche in Deutschland.
here

(kah-toh-lish-uh)
Ist das eine katholische Kirche?

(ay-vahn-gay-lish-uh)
Ist das eine evangelische Kirche?

(noy-uh)
Ist das eine neue Kirche?
new

(ahl-tuh)
Ist das eine alte Kirche?
old

Nun, let's learn how to say "I am" **auf Deutsch:** (eeH) (bin) **ich bin** _____
I am

Remember to breath hard when you say (eeH) „**ich.**" Test yourself — write each sentence on the

next page for more practice. Add your own personal variations as well.

Note that to use a feminine form of many words **auf Deutsch,** all you *generally* need to do is

add an "in." This will sometimes vary the pronounciation slightly.

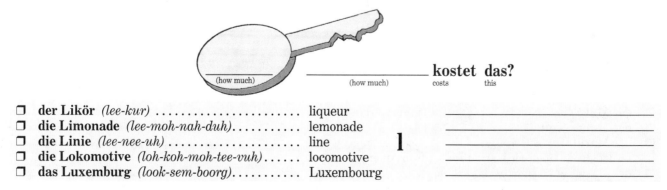

_____ **kostet das?**
(how much)   (how much)   costs   this

❐ **der Likör** *(lee-kur)* . . . . liqueur _____
❐ **die Limonade** *(lee-moh-nah-duh)* . . . . lemonade _____
❐ **die Linie** *(lee-nee-uh)* . . . . line _____
❐ **die Lokomotive** *(loh-koh-moh-tee-vuh)* . . . . . locomotive _____
❐ **das Luxemburg** *(look-sem-boorg)* . . . . Luxembourg _____

1

Ich bin katholisch. _(kah-toh-lish)_ _____

Ich bin evangelisch. _(ay-vahn-gay-lish)_ _____

Ich bin jüdisch. _(yew-dish)_ _____
Jewish

Ich bin Moslem. _(mohz-lem)_ _____

Ich bin Amerikaner. _(ah-mair-ih-kahn-air)_ _____
American (♂)

Ich bin Amerikanerin. _(ah-mair-ih-kahn-air-in)_ _____
American (♀)

Ich bin in der Kirche. _(kir-Huh)_ _____
I am in church

Ich bin in Europa. _(oy-roh-pah)_ _____

Ich bin in Deutschland. _(doych-lahnt)_ _____

Ich bin in dem Restaurant. _(dehm)_ _(res-toh-rahnt)_ _____

Ich bin Engländer. _(eng-len-dair)_ _____

Ich bin in dem Hotel. _(dehm)_ _____

Ich bin Kanadier. _(kah-nah-dyair)_ _____
Canadian (♂)

Ich bin Kanadierin. _(kah-nah-dyair-in)_ _____
Canadian (♀)

To negate any of these statements, simply add "<u>nicht</u>" _(neeHt)_ after the verb.
                                                      not

Ich bin <u>nicht</u> katholisch. _(neeHt)_ _____
I am not

Ich bin <u>nicht</u> Amerikaner. _____
I am not

Go through and drill all the above sentences again but with „nicht." _(neeHt)_

Nun, take a piece of paper. Our **Familie** _(fah-mee-lee-uh)_ from earlier had a reunion. Identify everyone below by writing **das richtige deutsche Wort** _(reeH-tee-guh)_ for each person — **die Mutter, den Onkel** _(moo-tair)_ _(ohn-kel)_ and
                                                correct
so on. Don't forget **den Hund!** _(hoont)_

❏ **der Mai** _(my)_ .... May
❏ **der Mann** _(mahn)_ .... man
❏ **der Markt** _(markt)_ .... market   **m**   _____
    usually an open air market in the town square _____
❏ **die Marmelade** _(mar-meh-lah-duh)_ .... marmalade, jam _____

12

(lair-nen)
Lernen!
to learn

You have already used **zwei** very important verbs: **ich möchte** *(murk-tuh)* and **ich habe** *(hah-buh)*. Although you *(tsvy)* — I would like — I have might be able to get by with only these verbs, let's assume you want to do better. First, a quick review.

How do you say ["I"] **auf Deutsch?** *(doych)* _____

How do you say ["we"] **auf Deutsch?** _____

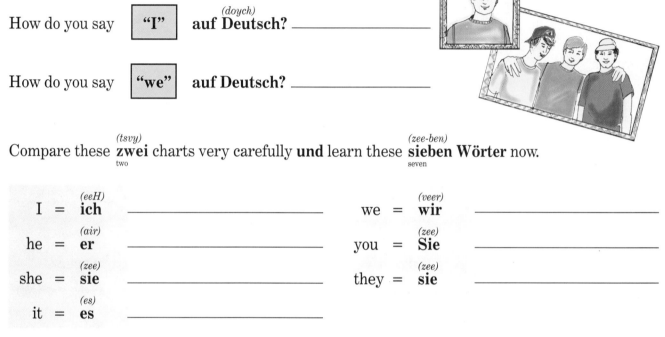

Compare these **zwei** *(tsvy)* charts very carefully **und** learn these **sieben Wörter** *(zee-ben)* now.
two   seven

I = **ich** *(eeH)* _____	we = **wir** *(veer)* _____
he = **er** *(air)* _____	you = **Sie** *(zee)* _____
she = **sie** *(zee)* _____	they = **sie** *(zee)* _____
it = **es** *(es)* _____	

Not too hard, is it? Draw lines between the matching **englische und deutsche Wörter** *(vur-tair)* below to see if you can keep these **Wörter** straight in your mind.

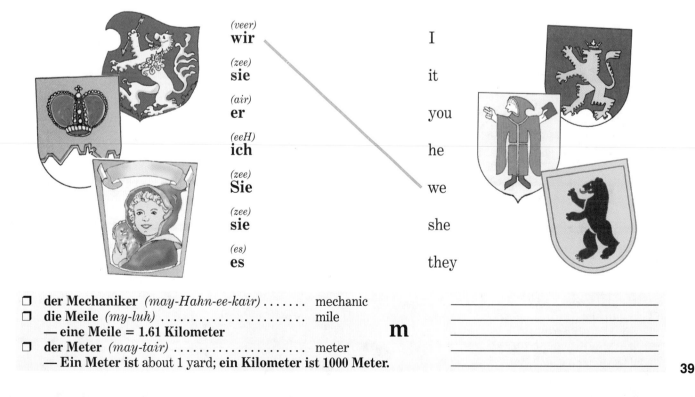

wir *(veer)*	I
sie *(zee)*	it
er *(air)*	you
ich *(eeH)*	he
Sie *(zee)*	we
sie *(zee)*	she
es *(es)*	they

❑ **der Mechaniker** *(may-Hahn-ee-kair)* .... mechanic
❑ **die Meile** *(my-luh)* .... mile
  — **eine Meile = 1.61 Kilometer**   **m**
❑ **der Meter** *(may-tair)* .... meter
  — **Ein Meter ist** about 1 yard; **ein Kilometer ist 1000 Meter.**

_____
_____
_____
_____

Nun close **das Buch und** write out both columns of this practice on **ein** *(shtewk)* **Stück** *(pah-peer)* **Papier.** How did
piece (of) paper

(zee) *(goot)* *(shlehHt)* *(zee)* *(zee)*
Sie do? **Gut oder schlecht? Nun** that **Sie** know these **Wörter, Sie** can say almost anything
well or poorly you you

auf Deutsch with one basic formula: the "plug-in" formula.

(zeks)
To demonstrate, let's take **sechs** basic **und** practical verbs **und** see how the "plug-in" formula
six

(zee) *(hah-ben)*
works. Write the verbs in the blanks after **Sie haben** practiced saying them out loud many times.
you have

(koh-men) *(gay-en)*
kommen _____ **gehen** _____
to come to go

(hah-ben) *(lair-nen)*
haben *haben, haben, haben* **lernen** _____
to have to learn

(brow-Hen) *(murk-ten)*
brauchen _____ **möchten** _____
to need would like

(zee)
Besides the familiar words already circled, can **Sie** find the above verbs in the puzzle below?

(zee)
When **Sie** find them, write them in the blanks to the right.

P	W	O	M	M	A	H	D	E	R	H
A	A	C	N	P	C	W	A	S	E	A
B	R	A	U	C	H	E	N	B	S	B
L	U	R	S	W	E	E	B	G	E	I
E	M	M	E	K	O	M	M	E	N	N
M	Ö	C	H	T	E	N	M	H	R	E
V	I	N	I	L	R	B	D	E	I	R
L	E	R	N	E	N	L	E	N	H	T

1. _____

2. _____

3. _____

4. _____

5. _____

6. _____

❐ **mehr** *(mair)* . . . . more
❐ **die Milch** *(milsh)* . . . . milk
❐ **die Mitte** *(mit-tuh)* . . . . middle   **m**
❐ **der Montag** *(mohn-tahk)* . . . . Monday
❐ **der Morgen** *(mor-gen)* . . . . morning

_____

_____

40

Study the following patterns carefully.

	(koh-muh) **komme**	= I *come*
	(gay-uh) **gehe**	= I *go*
(eeH) **ich** I	*(lair-nuh)* **lerne**	= I *learn*
	(brow-Huh) **brauche**	= I *need*
	(hah-buh) **habe**	= I *have*
	(murk-tuh) **möchte**	= I *would like*

	(kohmt) **kommt**	= he, she or it *comes*
	(gate) **geht**	= he, she or it *goes*
(air) **er** *(zee)* **sie** she *(es)* **es**	*(lairnt)* **lernt**	= he, she or it *learns*
	(browHt) **braucht**	= he, she or it *needs*
	(haht) **hat***	= he, she or it *has*
	(murk-tuh) **möchte***	= he, she or it *would like*

Note: • With all these verbs, the first thing you do is drop the final "**en**" from the basic

verb form or stem.

(eeH)
• With "**ich**," add "**e**" to the basic verb form.

(air) *(zee)*
• With "**er**," "**sie**," or "**es**," add "**t.**"

(murk-tuh)
• **Möchte** varies, but not too much. It is a very important verb so take a few extra

minutes to learn it

*Some verbs just will not conform to the pattern! But don't worry. Speak slowly **und** clearly,

und you will be perfectly understood whether you say „hat" or „haben." German speakers will

be delighted you have taken the time to learn their language.

Note: • German has three separate and very different ways of saying "you" whereas in

English we only use one word.

(zee)
• „**Sie**" will be used throughout this book and will be appropriate for most
you

(zee)
situations. „**Sie**" refers to both one or more persons in a formal sense.
you

(doo) *(ear)*
• „**Du**" and its plural form „**ihr**," are forms of address usually reserved for
you (singular)   you (plural)

family members, children, and very close friends.

❐	**der Mund** *(moont)*	mouth	
❐	**das Museum** *(moo-zay-oom)*	museum	**m**
❐	**die Musik** *(moo-zeek)*	music	
❐	**die Mutter** *(moo-tair)*	mother	**n**
❐	**nächst** *(nekst)*	next	

Here's your next group of patterns! With „ **wir,** " *(veer)* _{we} „ **Sie** " *(zee)* _{you} or „ **sie,** " *(zee)* _{they} there is no change at all!

(veer) **wir** *(zee)* **Sie** _{you} *(zee)* **sie** _{they} }	*(koh-men)* **kommen** = we, you, or they *come*	*(brow-Hen)* **brauchen** = we, you, or they *need*
	(gay-en) **gehen** = we, you, or they *go*	*(hah-ben)* **haben** = we, you, or they *have*
	(lair-nen) **lernen** = we, you, or they *learn*	*(murk-ten)* **möchten** = we, you, or they *would like*

Note: **Sie haben** only **zwei** *(tsvy)* changes to remember.

(eeH) **ich** ⟶ is followed by verbs with an "e" on the end . . . . *ex.* **ich brauch<u>e</u>**

(air) **er, sie, es** ⟶ are followed by verbs with a "t" on the end . . . . *ex.* **er brauch<u>t</u>**
sie brauch<u>t</u>
es brauch<u>t</u>

Hier sind sechs *(zeks)* more **Verben.** *(vair-ben)*
_{here} _{are} _{six} _{verbs}

(kow-fen) **kaufen** _____
_{to buy}

(voh-nen) **wohnen** __wohnen, wohnen__
_{to live, to reside}

(shpreh-Hen) **sprechen** _____
_{to speak}

(beh-shtel-len) **bestellen** _____
_{to order}

(bly-ben) **bleiben** _____
_{to stay, to remain}

(hi-sen) **heißen** _____
_{to be named}

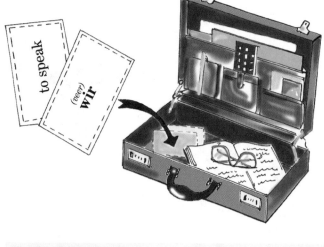

At the back of **das Buch,** *(booH)* **Sie** *(zee)* will find twelve

Seiten *(zy-ten)* of flash cards to help you learn these
_{pages}

neue Wörter. *(noy-uh)* Cut them out; carry them in
_{new}

your briefcase, purse, pocket **oder** *(oh-dair)* knapsack;
_{or}

review them whenever **Sie haben** *(hah-ben)* a free

moment.

❏	**die Nacht** *(nahHt)*	night	_____
	— **Gute Nacht!** *(goo-tuh)(nahHt)*	good night!	
❏	**der Name** *(nah-muh)*	name	**n** _____
❏	die Nation *(nah-tsee-ohn)*	nation	
❏	**die Nationalität** *(nah-tsee-oh-nahl-ih-tate)*	nationality	

Nun, it is your turn to practice what **Sie** *(zee)* have learned. Fill in the following blanks with the correct form of the verb. Each time **Sie** *(zee)* write out the sentence, be sure to say it aloud.

(koh-men)
kommen
to come

Ich _____ aus Amerika. *(ows) (ah-mair-ih-kah)* / from

Er
Sie _____ aus Kanada. *(kah-nah-dah)*
Es

Wir _____ aus Holland. *(hohl-lahnt)*

Sie _____ aus England. *(eng-lahnt)*
you

Sie _____ aus Deutschland.
they

(gay-en)
gehen
to go

Ich _____ morgen Abend. *(ah-bent)*

Er
Sie _____ ins Restaurant.
Es

Wir _____ mit dem Hund. *(mit) (hoont)* / with

Sie _____ heute Abend.
you

Sie _____ in die Küche.
they

(hah-ben)
haben
to have

Ich _____ zehn Euro. *(tsayn)*

Er
Sie _____ vierzig Euro. *(fear-tsig)*
Es

Wir _____ dreißig Euro. *(dry-sig)*

Sie _____ zwanzig Euro. *(tsvahn-tsig)*
you

Sie _____ hundert Euro. *(hoon-dairt)*
they

(lair-nen)
lernen
to learn

Ich _____ Deutsch. *(doych)*

Er
Sie _____ Japanisch. *(yah-pah-nish)*
Es

Wir _____ Italienisch. *(ee-tah-lee-ay-nish)*

Sie _____ Englisch. *(eng-lish)*
you

Sie _____ Spanisch. *(shpah-nish)*
they

(brow-Hen)
brauchen
to need

Ich _____ ein Zimmer. *(ein) (tsih-mair)*

Er
Sie _____ ein Glas Wasser. *(glahs) (vah-sair)* / glass water
Es

Wir _____ zwei Glas Wein. *(vine)* / wine

Sie _____ eine Tasse Tee. *(tah-suh) (tay)* / cup
you

Sie _____ vier Tassen Kaffee. *(fear) (kah-fay)*
they

(murk-ten)
möchten
would like

Ich _____ ein Glas Wein.

Er
Sie _____ eine Tasse Kakao. *(tah-suh) (kah-kow)* / cup   hot chocolate
Es

Wir _____ drei Glas Weißwein. *(vice-vine)* / white wine

Sie _____ ein Glas Milch. *(milsh)*
you

Sie _____ zwei Glas Bier. *(tsvy)*
they

❑ **natürlich** *(nah-tewr-leeH)*	naturally	
❑ **der November** *(noh-vem-bair)*	November	**n**
❑ **die Nummer** *(noo-mair)*	number	
❑ **der Ofen** *(oh-fen)*	oven	**o**
❑ **oft** *(ohft)*	often	

_____
_____
_____
_____
_____

Now take a break, walk around the room, take a deep breath **und** do the next *(zeks)* **sechs** verbs.

(kow-fen)
kaufen
to buy

Ich _____ ein Buch. *(booH)*

Er
Sie _____ einen Salat. *(eye-nen) (zah-laht)*
Es

Wir _____ ein Auto. *(ow-toh)*

Sie _____ eine Uhr. *(eye-nuh) (oor)*
you

Sie _____ sieben Karten. *(zee-ben) (kar-ten)*
they
tickets

(beh-shtel-len)
bestellen
to order

Ich _____ ein Glas Wasser. *(glahs) (vah-sair)*
water

Er
Sie _____ ein Glas Wein. *(vine)*
Es

Wir _____ zwei Tassen Tee. *(tah-sen) (tay)*

Sie _____ eine Tasse Kaffee. *(kah-fay)*
you

Sie _____ drei Tassen Tee. *(dry)*
they

(voh-nen)
wohnen
to live, to reside

Ich _____ in Deutschland. *(doych-lahnt)*

Er
Sie _____ in Amerika. *(ah-mair-ih-kah)*
Es

Wir _____ in einem Hotel. *(eye-nem)*

Sie _____ in Europa. *(oy-roh-pah)*
you

Sie _____ in Japan. *(yah-pahn)*
they

(bly-ben)
bleiben
to stay, to remain

Ich _____ noch fünf Tage. *(nohH) (fewnf) (tah-guh)*
still
days

Er
Sie _____ noch drei Tage. *(nohH) (dry)*
Es

Wir _____ in Deutschland. *(doych-lahnt)*

Sie _____ in Berlin. *(bair-leen)*
you

Sie _____ in Frankfurt. *(frahnk-foort)*
they

(shpreh-Hen)
sprechen
to speak

Ich sprechen Deutsch.

Ich _____ Deutsch. *(doych)*

Er
Sie spricht / _____ Englisch. *(eng-lish)*
Es

Wir _____ Spanisch. *(shpah-nish)*

Sie _____ Dänisch. *(day-nish)*
you

Sie _____ Japanisch. *(yah-pah-nish)*
they

(hi-sen)
heißen
to be called

Ich heiße Karla.

Ich _____ Doktor Müller. *(dohk-tor) (mew-lair)*

Er
Sie _____ Zimmermann. *(tsih-mair-mahn)*
Es

Wir _____ Faber. *(fah-bair)*

Sie _____ Seehafer. *(zay-hah-fair)*
you

Sie _____ Familie Nickel. *(fah-mee-lee-uh)*
they

❏ **offen** *(ohf-fen)* . . . . open
  — **Das Restaurant ist offen.**
❏ **offiziell** *(oh-fee-tsee-el)* . . . . official
❏ **der Offizier** *(oh-fee-tseer)* . . . . officer
❏ **der Oktober** *(ohk-toh-bair)* . . . . October

O _____
_____
_____
_____

Ja, *(yah)* yes it is hard to get used to all those new words. Just keep practicing **und** before **Sie** *(zee)* know

it, **Sie** will be using them naturally. **Nun** *(noon)* is a perfect time to turn to the back of this **Buch,** clip

out your verb flash cards **und** start flashing. Don't skip over your free **Wörter** either. Check

them off in the box provided as **Sie lernen** *(lair-nen)* learn each one. See if **Sie** can fill in the blanks below. **Die**

richtigen Antworten sind *(ahnt-vor-ten)* at the bottom of the **Seite.** *(zy-tuh)* page

1. _____
(I speak German.)

2. _____
(We learn German.)

3. _____
(She needs 10 Euro.)

4. _____
(He comes from Canada.)

5. _____
(They live in Germany.)

6. _____
(You buy a book.)

In the following Steps, **Sie** *(zee)* will be introduced

to more verbs **und Sie** should drill them

in exactly the same way as **Sie** did in this

section. Look up **die neuen Wörter** *(dee) (noy-en)* new in your

Wörterbuch und *(vur-tair-booH)* dictionary make up your own

sentences. Try out your **neue Wörter** *(noy-uh)* for

that's how you make them yours to use on

your holiday. Remember, the more **Sie**

practice **jetzt,** *(yets-t)* now the more enjoyable your trip

will be. **Viel Glück!** *(feel) (glewk)* good luck

13

(vee) (feel) (oor)
Wie viel Uhr ist es?
what time is it

(zee) Sie know how to tell die **Tage** *(tah-guh)* of the **Woche und die** *(voh-Huh)* **Monate** *(moh-nah-tuh)* of the **Jahr,** *(yar)* so let's learn to tell
days   week   months   year

time. Punctuality **in Deutschland ist sehr** *(zair)* **wichtig,** *(veeH-teeg)* plus **Sie** need to be able to tell time in order
very   important

to make **Reservierungen, und** *(rez-air-veer-oong-en)* to catch **Züge** *(tsue-guh)* **und Busse.** *(boo-suh)* **Hier sind** the basics.
reservations   trains   here   are

What time is it?	=	**Wie viel Uhr ist es?** *(vee) (feel) (oor) (ist) (es)* _____
noon	=	**Mittag** *(mit-tahk)* _____
midnight	=	**Mitternacht** *(mit-tair-nahHt)* _____
half	=	**halb** *(hahlp)* _____
before/to	=	**vor** *(for)* _____
after	=	**nach** *(nahH)* _____
a quarter	=	**ein Viertel** *(ein) (fear-tel)* _____
a quarter to	=	**Viertel vor** *(for)* _____
a quarter after	=	**Viertel nach** *(fear-tel) (nahH)* _____

Nun quiz yourself. Fill in the missing letters below.

noon = | M | | t | | g | before / to = | v | | |

a quarter = | e | | n | ✕ | V | | r | | e | l |

half = | h | a | | | after = | n | a | | |

And finally, midnight = | M | | t | | | n | | c | | t |

❑ **das Ohr** *(or)* . . . . ear   _____
❑ **der Ohrring** *(or-ring)* . . . . earring   _____
❑ **das Öl** *(url)* . . . . oil   **o** _____
❑ das Omelett *(oh-meh-let)* . . . . omelette   _____
❑ **der Onkel** *(ohn-kel)* . . . . uncle

Nun, wie sind these **Wörter** used? Study the examples below. When **Sie** think it through,

(vee) (zint)
how

it really is not too difficult. Just notice that the pattern changes after the halfway mark.

Es ist fünf Uhr. `5:00` Es ist fünf Uhr.
(fewnf)
it   five o'clock

Es ist zehn nach fünf. `5:10`
(tsayn) (nahH)

Es ist Viertel nach fünf. `5:15`
(fear-tel)

Es ist zwanzig nach fünf. `5:20`
(tsvahn-tsig)

Es ist halb sechs. `5:30`
(hahlp) (zeks)
half   six

Es ist zwanzig vor sechs. `5:40`
(for)

Es ist Viertel vor sechs. `5:45`

Es ist zehn vor sechs. `5:50`
(tsayn)

Es ist sechs Uhr. `6:00`
(oor)

See how **wichtig** it is to learn **die Nummern?** Answer the following **Fragen** based on the
(veeH-teeg)   *(noo-mairn)*   *(frah-gen)*
questions

Uhren below. **Wie viel Uhr ist es?**
(vee) (feel)
clocks

1. `8:00` _____

2. `7:15` _____

3. `4:30` _____

4. `9:20` _____

47

When **Sie** answer a „**Wann?**" *(vahn)* question, say „**um**" *(oom)* before **Sie** give the time.

when .... *at*

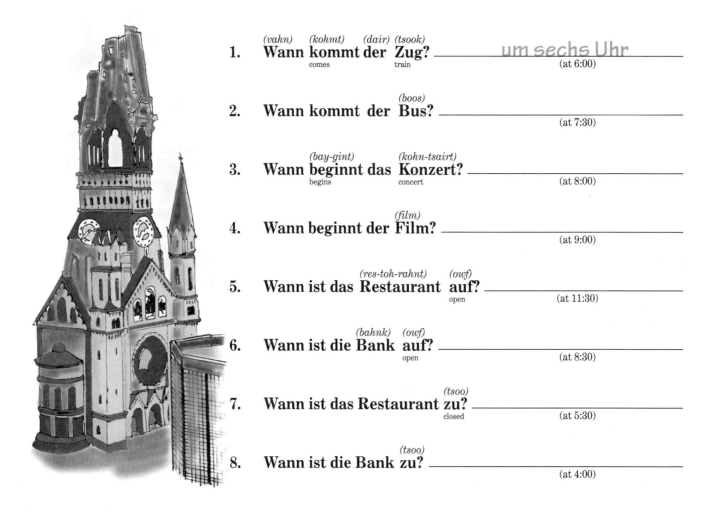

1. **Wann kommt der Zug?** _____um sechs Uhr_____
   (vahn) (kohmt) (dair) (tsook)
   comes .... train .... (at 6:00)

2. **Wann kommt der Bus?** _____
   (boos)
   .... (at 7:30)

3. **Wann beginnt das Konzert?** _____
   (bay-gint) (kohn-tsairt)
   begins .... concert .... (at 8:00)

4. **Wann beginnt der Film?** _____
   (film)
   .... (at 9:00)

5. **Wann ist das Restaurant auf?** _____
   (res-toh-rahnt) (owf)
   open .... (at 11:30)

6. **Wann ist die Bank auf?** _____
   (bahnk) (owf)
   open .... (at 8:30)

7. **Wann ist das Restaurant zu?** _____
   (tsoo)
   closed .... (at 5:30)

8. **Wann ist die Bank zu?** _____
   (tsoo)
   .... (at 4:00)

Hier ist a quick quiz. Fill in the blanks **mit den richtigen Nummern.**
(dehn) (reeH-tee-gen) (noo-mairn)
with

9. **Eine Minute hat** _____ **Sekunden.**
   (mee-noo-tuh) (haht) .... *(zay-koon-den)*
   minute .... has .... (?) .... seconds

10. **Eine Stunde hat** _____ **Minuten.**
    (shtoon-duh) .... *(mee-noo-ten)*
    hour .... (?) .... minutes

11. **Eine Woche hat** _____ **Tage.**
    (voh-Huh) (haht) .... *(tah-guh)*
    week .... (?) .... days

12. **Ein Jahr hat** _____ **Monate.**
    (yar) .... *(moh-nah-tuh)*
    year .... (?) .... months

13. **Ein Jahr hat** _____ **Wochen.**
    (voh-Hen)
    .... (?) .... weeks

14. **Ein Jahr hat** _____ **Tage.**
    .... (?)

ANTWORTEN

14. dreihundertfünfundsechzig
13. zweiundfünfzig
12. zwölf
11. sieben
10. sechzig
9. sechzig
8. um vier Uhr

7. um halb sechs
6. um halb neun
5. um halb zwölf
4. um neun Uhr
3. um acht Uhr
2. um halb acht
1. um sechs Uhr

Do **Sie** *(zee)* remember your greetings from earlier? It is a good time to review them as they will

always be **sehr** *(zair)* **wichtig** *(veeH-teeg)*.
very   important

Um acht Uhr *(oom)* **morgens** *(mor-gens)* **sagt** *(zahkt)* **man** *(mahn)*, „Guten **Morgen** *(goo-ten)*, **Frau** *(frow)* **Bernhard** *(bairn-hart)*!"
at   in the morning   says   one   good   morning   Mrs.

Was *(vahs)* **sagt** *(zahkt)* **man?** _____ Guten Morgen, Frau Bernhard!
what   does one say

Um ein Uhr *(ein)* **nachmittags** *(nahH-mit-tahks)* **sagt man** *(zahkt)*, „Guten **Tag** *(tahk)*, **Herr** *(hair)* **Richter** *(reeH-tair)*!"
one   in the afternoon   Mr.

Was *(vahs)* **sagt** *(zahkt)* **man?** *(mahn)* _____

Um acht Uhr abends *(ah-bents)* **sagt man** *(zahkt)*, „Guten **Abend** *(ah-bent)*, **Frau** *(frow)* **Seehafer** *(zay-hah-fair)*."
in the evening   Ms. / Mrs.

Was *(vahs)* **sagt man?** _____

Um zehn Uhr abends sagt man, „Gute **Nacht** *(goo-tuh) (nahHt)*."
ten

Was sagt man? *(mahn)* _____
one

Sie have probably already noticed that plurals are formed in a variety of ways.

SINGULAR	PLURAL
die Frau	→ die Frau**en**
die Postkarte	→ die Postkarte**n**
der Tisch	→ die Tisch**e**
das Auto	→ die Auto**s**
der Mann	→ die M**ä**nn**er** *(dee) (men-air)*

Know that **deutsche Wörter** change their endings in the plural so always listen for the core of

the word.

❐ **die Oper** *(oh-pair)* . . . . opera _____
— **Ich gehe in die Oper.**
❐ **das Opernhaus** *(oh-pairn-house)* . . . . opera house **o** _____
— **Das Opernhaus ist sehr alt.** _____
❐ **die Ordnung** *(ord-noong)* . . . . order _____

49

Hier sind zwei neue Verben für Sie.

(noy-uh) *(fewr)*

(ess-en)
essen _____
to eat

(trink-en)
trinken _____
to drink

(ess-en)
essen
to eat

(trink-en)
trinken
to drink

(vee-nair) *(shnit-tsel)*
Ich _____ **Wiener Schnitzel.**

Er
Sie _isst /_ _____ **Fisch.** *(fish)*
Es

Wir _____ **viel.** *(feel)*
a lot

Sie _____ **ein Beefsteak.**
you

Sie _____ **Lamm.** *(lahm)*
lamb

(milsh)
Ich _____ **Milch.**

Er
Sie _trinkt /_ _____ **nichts.** *(neeH-ts)*
Es nothing

Wir _____ **Mineralwasser.** *(mih-nair-ahl-vah-sair)*

Sie _____ **Tomatensaft.** *(toh-mah-ten-zahft)*
tomato juice

Sie _____ **Kakao.** *(kah-kow)*
they hot chocolate

Remember that „a" sounds like "ah." Practice **Land**, **schlafen**, **baden**, **danke**, **was**, **wann**
(lahnt) *(shlah-fen)* *(bah-den)* *(dahn-kuh)*

and **Bank**. Also „au" is pronounced "ow" as in "Wow!" Practice **Frau**, **auf**, **kaufen**, **August**
(bahnk) *(owf)* *(kow-fen)* *(ow-goost)*

and **aus**.
(ows)

❑ **das Orchester** *(or-kes-tair)* .... orchestra _____
— **Das Orchester in Berlin ist sehr gut.**
❑ **die Organisation** *(or-gahn-ih-zah-tsee-ohn)*.. organization _____
❑ **die Orgel** *(or-gel)* .... organ
— **Die Orgel ist nicht neu.**

50

Sie haben *(hah-ben)* learned a lot of material in the last few steps **und** that means it is time to quiz yourself. Don't panic, this is just for you **und** no one else needs to know how **Sie** did. Remember, this is a chance to review, find out what **Sie** remember **und** what **Sie** need to spend more time on. After **Sie** have finished, check your **Antworten** in the glossary at the back of this book. Circle the correct answers.

der Kaffee	tea	coffee		**die Familie**	seven	family
ja	yes	no		**die Kinder**	children	grandfather
die Tante	aunt	uncle		**die Milch**	butter	(milk)
oder	and	or		**das Salz**	pepper	salt
lernen	to drink	to learn		**über**	under	over
die Nacht	morning	night		**der Mann**	man	doctor
Freitag	Friday	Tuesday		**der Juni**	June	July
sprechen	to live	to speak		**die Küche**	kitchen	religions
der Winter	summer	winter		**ich habe**	I want	I have
das Geld	money	page		**kaufen**	to order	to buy
zehn	nine	ten		**gestern**	yesterday	tomorrow
viel	a lot	bread		**gut**	good	yellow

(vee) (gate) (ee-nen)
Wie geht es Ihnen?   <u>What time is it?</u>   <u>How are you?</u>   Well, how are you after this quiz?

❐ **der Ozean** *(oh-tsay-ahn)* . . . . ocean

— **Der Ozean ist blau und grün.**   **o** _____

❐ **ein Paar** *(ein)(par)* . . . . a pair, a couple   _____

❐ **packen** *(pah-ken)* . . . . to pack   **p** _____

❐ **das Paket** *(pah-kate)* . . . . package   _____

51

(nort) *(zewt)* *(ohst)* *(vest)*

Nord - Süd, Ost - West
north   south   east   west

If **Sie** are looking at **eine Landkarte und Sie** see the following **Wörter,** it should not be too
(lahnt-kar-tuh)
map

difficult to figure out what they mean. Take an educated guess.

(nort-ah-mair-ih-kah)
das Nordamerika

(nort-pohl)
der Nordpol

(zewt-ah-mair-ih-kah)
das Südamerika

(zewt-pohl)
der Südpol

(ohst-kews-tuh)
die Ostküste

(nort-zay)
die Nordsee

(vest-kews-tuh)
die Westküste

(zewt-ah-frih-kah)
das Südafrika

Die deutschen Wörter für "north," "south," "east," **und** "west" are easy to recognize due to
(fewr)

their similarity to **Englisch**. These **Wörter sind sehr wichtig**. Learn them **jetzt!**
(zair) *(veeH-teeg)* *(yets-t)*
are

(nort)
nord _____
north

(vest)
west _____
west

(ohst)
ost _____
east

(zewt)
süd _____
south

(links)
links
left

(geh-rah-duh-ows)
geradeaus

(rehH-ts)
rechts

_____ (left)   _____ (straight ahead)   _____ (right)

ANTWORTEN

South Africa	west coast
North Sea	east coast
North Pole, South Pole	South America
North Pole	North America

These **Wörter** can go a long way. Say them aloud each time you write them in the blanks below.

(bit-tuh)
bitte _____
please

(dahn-kuh)
danke _____
thank you

(ent-shool-dee-goong)   *(fair-tsy-oong)*
Entschuldigung / Verzeihung _____
excuse me

(bit-tuh)
bitte _____
you're welcome

           (tsvy) *(zair)* *(too-pish-uh)* *(kohn-vair-zah-tsee-oh-nen)(fewr)*
Hier sind zwei sehr typische Konversationen für someone who is trying to find something.
                              typical   conversations

Write them out in the blanks below.

Karl:
   (ent-shool-dee-goong)   *(rit-tair)*
   Entschuldigung. Wo ist das Hotel Ritter?
                                  knight

Entschuldigung. Wo ist das Hotel Ritter?

Heinz:
   (gay-en)   *(shtrah-sen)* *(vy-tair)* *(dahn)*
   Gehen Sie zwei Straßen weiter, dann links.
   go   streets   further   then

_____

                      (owf)   *(rehH-ten)*   *(zy-tuh)*
   Das Hotel Ritter ist auf der rechten Seite.
                    on   right   side

_____

Thomas:
   (ent-shool-dee-goong)   *(moo-zay-oom)*
   Entschuldigung. Wo ist das Deutsche Museum?

_____

Helga:
   (gay-en)   *(geh-rah-duh-ows)* *(oon-geh-fair)*   *(vy-tair)*
   Gehen Sie geradeaus. Ungefähr hundert Meter weiter
             straight ahead   approximately

_____

   (owf)   *(zy-tuh)*
   auf der linken Seite ist das Deutsche Museum.
   on

_____

❐ **das Papier** *(pah-peer)* .... paper   _____
❐ **der Park** *(park)* .... park   _____
❐ **der Passagier** *(pah-sah-zheer)* .... passenger   **p**   _____
❐ **der Pass** *(pahss)*...................... passport   _____
❐ **die Passkontrolle** *(pahss-kohn-trohl-luh)*... passport control, check _____

Are **Sie** *(zee)* lost? There is no need to be lost if **Sie haben** *(hah-ben)* learned the basic direction **Wörter.** Do not

try to memorize these **Konversationen** because **Sie** will never be looking for precisely these

places. One day, **Sie** might need to ask directions to „das **Goethe** *(guh-tuh)* **Museum**" or „das **Hotel**

Europa." *(oy-roh-pah)* Learn the key direction **Wörter und** be sure **Sie** can find your destination. **Sie** may

want to buy a guidebook to start planning which places **Sie** would like to visit. Practice asking

directions to these special places. What if the person responding to your **Frage** *(frah-guh)* answers too (question)

quickly for **Sie** to understand the entire reply? Practice saying,

Entschuldigung. Ich verstehe *(fair-shtay-uh)* **nicht.** *(neeHt)* **Wiederholen** *(vee-dair-hoh-len)* **Sie das bitte.**

do not understand   repeat   that

Nun, say it again **und** then write it out below.

_____

(Excuse me. I do not understand. Please repeat that.)

Ja, *(yah)* **es ist schwer** *(shvair)* at first but don't give up! When the directions are repeated, **Sie** will be able to

yes   difficult

understand if **Sie haben** learned the key **Wörter.** Let's review by writing them in the blanks below.

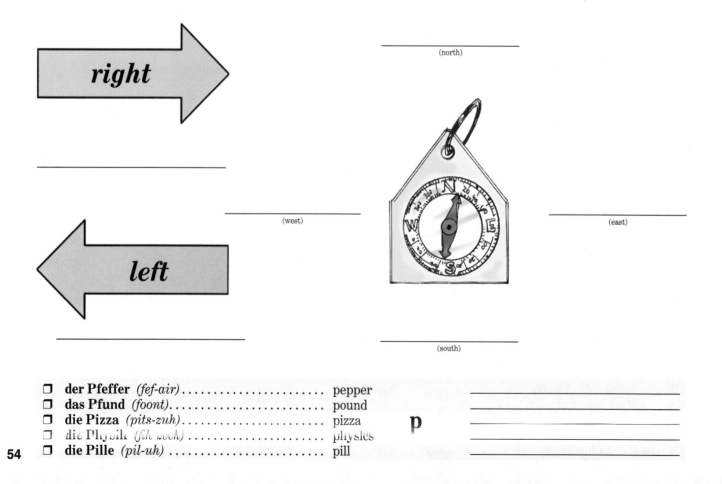

right

left

_____ (north)

_____ (west)

_____ (east)

_____ (south)

❐ **der Pfeffer** *(fef-air)*	pepper		_____
❐ **das Pfund** *(foont)*	pound		_____
❐ **die Pizza** *(pits-zuh)*	pizza	**p**	_____
❐ die Physik *(fü-zeek)*	physics		_____
❐ **die Pille** *(pil-uh)*	pill		_____

(fear)

Hier sind vier neue Verben.

(zah-gen)
sagen _____
to say

(fair-shtay-en)
verstehen _____
to understand

(fair-kow-fen)
verkaufen _____
to sell

(vee-dair-hoh-len)
wiederholen _____
to repeat

As always, say each sentence out loud. Say each **und** every *(vort)* **Wort** carefully, pronouncing each

German sound as well as **Sie** can.

(zah-gen)
sagen
to say

> Guten Tag!

Ich _____ „Guten Tag."

Er
Sie _____ „nein."
Es *(nine)* no

Wir _____ „Gute Nacht."

Sie _____ „ja."
you

Sie _____ nichts.
(neeH-ts) nothing

(fair-shtay-en)
verstehen
to understand

> Ich verstehe Deutsch.

Ich _____ Englisch.

Er
Sie versteht / _____ Italienisch.
Es *(ee-tah-lee-ay-nish)*

Wir _____ Deutsch.

Sie _____ Russisch.
(roo-sish) Russian

Sie _____ Dänisch.
they *(day-nish)* Danish

(fair-kow-fen)
verkaufen
to sell

Ich _____ Blumen.
(bloo-men)

Er
Sie _____ nichts.
Es *(neeH-ts)* nothing

Wir _____ Postkarten.

Sie _____ Wein und Bier.
you *(vine)*

Sie _____ Briefmarken.
(breef-mar-ken) stamps

(vee-dair-hoh-len)
wiederholen
to repeat

> Bitte? Bitte? Bitte?

Ich _____ das Wort.

Er
Sie _____ die Frage.
Es *(frah-guh)* question

Wir _____ die Namen.
names

Sie _____ die Antworten.
answers

Sie _____ die Adresse.
they *(ah-dres-suh)*

❏ **das Polen** *(poh-len)* .... Poland
  — **wo sie Polnisch sprechen** *(pohl-nish)*
❏ **die Police** *(poh-lee-suh)* .... policy (insurance)   **p** _____
❏ **die Polizei** *(poh-lih-tsy)* .... police   _____
❏ **die Politik** *(poh-lih-teek)* .... politics

(oh-ben)
Oben – Unten
(oon-ten)

above / upstairs   below / downstairs

(noon) *(lair-nen)* *(vir)* *(mair)*
Nun lernen wir mehr Wörter. Hier ist ein Haus in Deutschland. Gehen Sie in your
        more   *(doych-lahnt)* *(gay-en)*
house

(shlahf-tsih-mair) *(tsih-mair)* *(nah-men)*
Schlafzimmer und look around **das Zimmer.** Let's learn **die Namen** of the **Dinge in dem**
bedroom   room   names

(tsih-mair)
Zimmer, just like **wir** learned the various parts of the **Haus.**

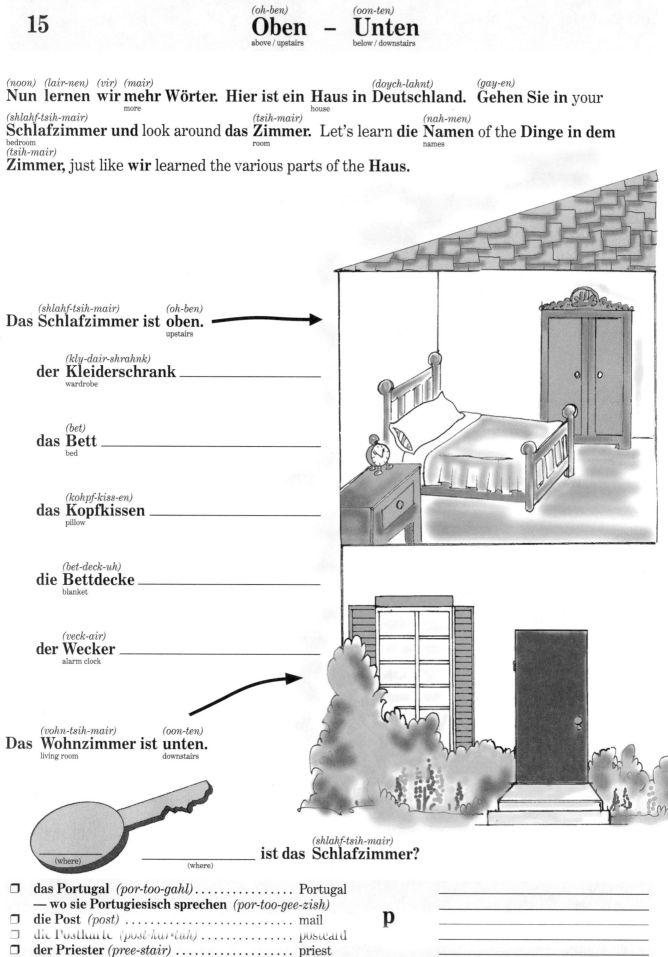

(shlahf-tsih-mair)   *(oh-ben)*
Das Schlafzimmer ist oben.
                   upstairs

(kly-dair-shrahnk)
der Kleiderschrank _____
wardrobe

(bet)
das Bett _____
bed

(kohpf-kiss-en)
das Kopfkissen _____
pillow

(bet-deck-uh)
die Bettdecke _____
blanket

(veck-air)
der Wecker _____
alarm clock

(vohn-tsih-mair)   *(oon-ten)*
Das Wohnzimmer ist unten.
living room   downstairs

_____ (where)
                (shlahf-tsih-mair)
_____ **ist das Schlafzimmer?**
(where)

❐ **das Portugal** *(por-too-gahl)* . . . . Portugal   _____
— **wo sie Portugiesisch sprechen** *(por-too-gee-zish)*   _____
❐ **die Post** *(post)* . . . . mail   **p**   _____
❐ **die Postkarte** *(post-kar-tuh)* . . . . postcard   _____
❐ **der Priester** *(pree-stair)* . . . . priest

Jetzt, remove the next **fünf** stickers **und** label these things **in** your **Schlafzimmer**. Let's move *(yets-t)* *(fewnf)* *(shlahf-tsih-mair)*

now

into **das Badezimmer und** do the same thing. Remember, **das Badezimmer** means a room to *(bah-duh-tsih-mair)* *(bah-duh-tsih-mair)*

bathroom

bathe in. If **Sie sind in einem Restaurant und Sie** need to use the lavatory, **Sie** want to ask for *(zee)* *(zint)*

die Toilette und *not* for **das Badezimmer**. Restrooms may be marked with pictures *(toy-let-tuh)*

oder simply the letters **D oder H**. Don't confuse them!

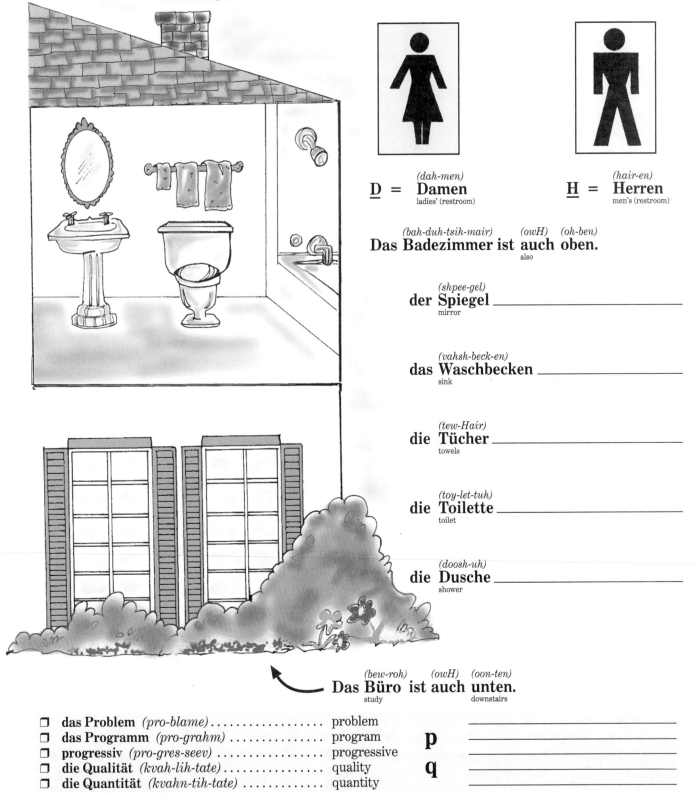

D = **Damen** *(dah-men)*
ladies' (restroom)

H = **Herren** *(hair-en)*
men's (restroom)

Das Badezimmer ist auch oben. *(bah-duh-tsih-mair)* *(owH)* *(oh-ben)*

also

der Spiegel _____ *(shpee-gel)*
mirror

das Waschbecken _____ *(vahsh-beck-en)*
sink

die Tücher _____ *(tew-Hair)*
towels

die Toilette _____ *(toy-let-tuh)*
toilet

die Dusche _____ *(doosh-uh)*
shower

Das Büro ist auch unten. *(bew-roh)* *(owH)* *(oon-ten)*

study   downstairs

❏ **das Problem** *(pro-blame)* .... problem
❏ **das Programm** *(pro-grahm)* .... program
❏ **progressiv** *(pro-gres-seev)* .... progressive
❏ **die Qualität** *(kvah-lih-tate)* .... quality
❏ **die Quantität** *(kvahn-tih-tate)* .... quantity

p _____

q _____

Do not forget to remove the next group of stickers **und** label these things in your **Haus.** Okay, it is time to review. Here's a quick quiz to see what you remember.

men's (restroom)   *(oon-ten)* **unten**

I understand   *(hair-en)* **Herren**

downstairs   *(bit-tuh)* **bitte**

please   *(fair-shtay-uh)* **ich verstehe**

towels   *(bah-duh-tsih-mair)* **das Badezimmer**

upstairs   *(geh-rah-duh-ows)* **geradeaus**

bathroom   *(dah-men)* **Damen**

lavatory / restroom   *(tew-Hair)* **die Tücher**

straight ahead   *(oh-ben)* **oben**

women's (restroom)   *(toy-let-tuh)* **die Toilette**

❏ **radikal** *(rah-dee-kahl)* . . . . radical   _____
❏ **das Radio** *(rah-dee-oh)* . . . . radio   _____
❏ **recht** *(rehHt)* . . . . right, correct   **r** _____
❏ **die Religion** *(ray-lee-gee-ohn)* . . . . religion   _____
58 ❏ **das Restaurant** *(res-toh-rahnt)* . . . . restaurant   _____

Next stop — **das Büro,** *(bew-roh)* office specifically **der Tisch** *(tish)* table **oder der Schreibtisch in dem Büro.** *(shripe-tish)* desk *(bew-roh)* **Was ist auf** *(vahs)* what *(owf)* on *(dehm)* **dem Tisch?** Let's identify **die Dinge** which one normally finds **in dem Büro** *(bew-roh)* **oder** strewn about things

das Haus.

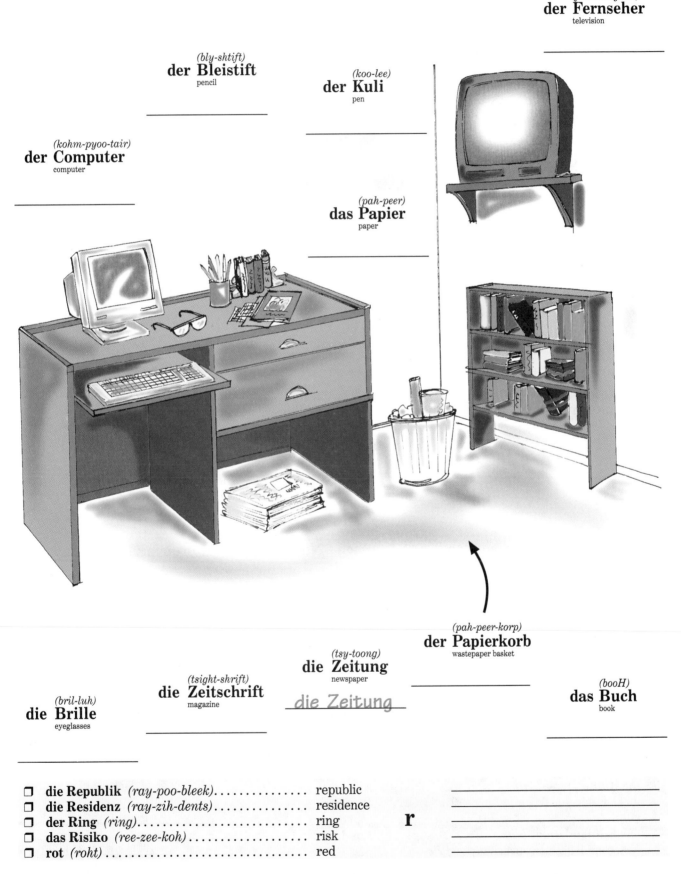

der Fernseher *(fairn-zay-air)* television

der Bleistift *(bly-shtift)* pencil

der Kuli *(koo-lee)* pen

der Computer *(kohm-pyoo-tair)* computer

das Papier *(pah-peer)* paper

der Papierkorb *(pah-peer-korp)* wastepaper basket

die Zeitung *(tsy-toong)* newspaper

die Zeitung

die Zeitschrift *(tsight-shrift)* magazine

die Brille *(bril-luh)* eyeglasses

das Buch *(booH)* book

r

Don't forget these essentials!

(breef)
der Brief
letter

(breef-mar-kuh)
die Briefmarke
stamp

(post-kar-tuh)
die Postkarte
postcard

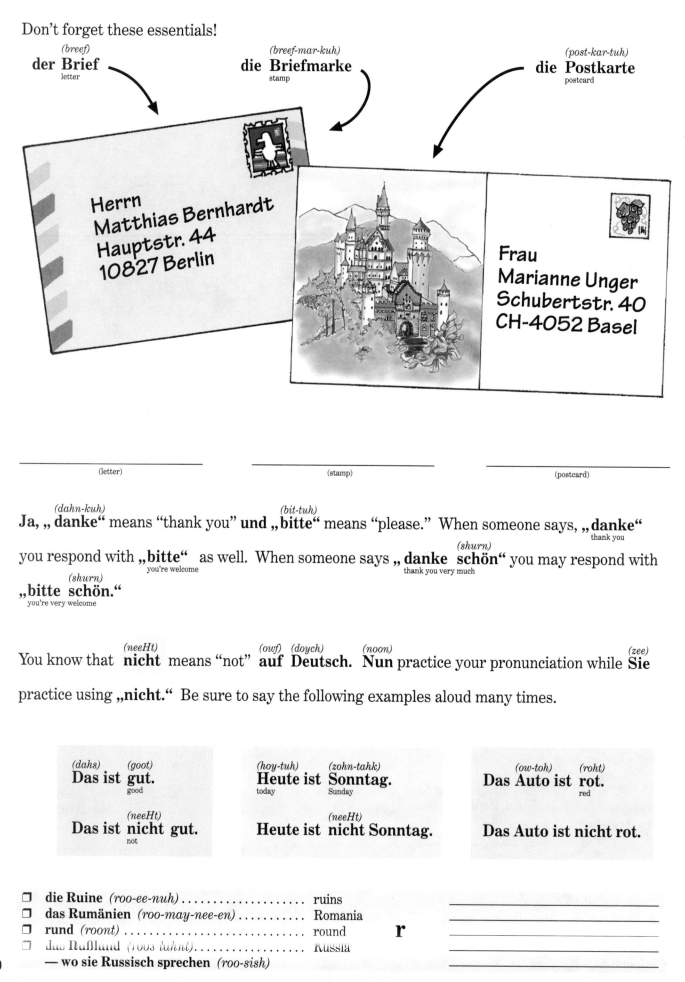

Herrn
Matthias Bernhardt
Hauptstr. 44
10827 Berlin

Frau
Marianne Unger
Schubertstr. 40
CH-4052 Basel

_____   _____   _____
(letter)   (stamp)   (postcard)

(dahn-kuh)   *(bit-tuh)*
Ja, „danke" means "thank you" **und „bitte"** means "please." When someone says, **„danke"**
thank you

you respond with **„bitte"** as well. When someone says **„danke schön"** you may respond with
you're welcome   *(shurn)*
                                                   thank you very much

(shurn)
„bitte schön."
you're very welcome

(neeHt)   *(owf) (doych)*   *(noon)*   *(zee)*
You know that **nicht** means "not" **auf Deutsch.** **Nun** practice your pronunciation while **Sie**

practice using **„nicht."** Be sure to say the following examples aloud many times.

(dahs) *(goot)*
Das ist gut.
good

(neeHt)
Das ist nicht gut.
not

(hoy-tuh) *(zohn-tahk)*
Heute ist Sonntag.
today   Sunday

(neeHt)
Heute ist nicht Sonntag.

(ow-toh) *(roht)*
Das Auto ist rot.
red

Das Auto ist nicht rot.

❏ **die Ruine** *(roo-ee-nuh)* . . . . ruins   _____
❏ **das Rumänien** *(roo-may-nee-en)* . . . . Romania   _____
❏ **rund** *(roont)* . . . . round   **r**   _____
❏ **das Rußland** *(roos-lahnt)* . . . . Russia   _____
— **wo sie Russisch sprechen** *(roo-sish)*

Simple, isn't it? **Nun,** *(noon)* after you fill in the blanks below, go back a second time and negate all these sentences by adding „**nicht**." Don't get discouraged! Just look at how much **Sie** have already learned **und** think ahead to wonderful food, **das Oktoberfest** *(ohk-toh-bair-fest)* **und** new adventures.

(zay-en)
sehen
to see
_____

(shlah-fen)
schlafen
to sleep
_____

(shick-en)
schicken
to send
_____

(fin-den)
finden
to find
_____

(zay-en)
sehen
to see

Ich _____ das **Museum.** *(moo-zay-oom)*

Er
Sie *sieht /* _____ die **Stadt.** *(shtaht)* city
Es

Wir _____ die **Alpen.** *(ahl-pen)* Alps

Sie _____ das **Schloss.** *(shlohss)* you / castle

Sie _____ die **Kirche.**

(shlah-fen)
schlafen
to sleep

Ich _____ im **Schlafzimmer.** *(shlahf-tsih-mair)*

Er
Sie *schläft /* _____ im **Hotel.**
Es

Wir _____ im **Hause.** *(how-zuh)*

Sie _____ mit **Bettdecken.** *(bet-deck-en)* blankets

Sie _____ ohne **Bettdecken.** *(oh-nuh)* they / without

(shick-en)
schicken
to send

Ich _____ den **Brief.** *(breef)*

Er
Sie *schickt /* _____ die **Postkarte.**
Es

Wir _____ das **Buch.** *(booH)*

Sie _____ drei **Postkarten.**

Sie _____ vier **Briefe.** they

(fin-den)
finden
to find

Ich _____ das **Restaurant.**

Er
Sie *findet /* _____ das **Hotel.**
Es

Wir _____ die **Brille.**

Sie _____ das **Museum.** *(moo-zay-oom)* you

Sie _____ das **Rathaus.** *(raht-house)* city hall

❏ **der Salat** *(zah-laht)*	salad	**S** _____
❏ **das Salz** *(zahlts)*	salt	_____
❏ **sauer** *(zow-air)*	sour (vs. sweet = **süß**)	_____
❏ **scharf** *(sharf)*	sharp (spicy)	_____
❏ **der Scheck** *(sheck)*	check	_____

Before **Sie** proceed **mit** the next step, **bitte** identify all the items **unten.** *(oon-ten)*

die **Zeitung** *(tsy-toong)*

der **Papierkorb** *(pah-peer-korp)*

die **Postkarte**

das **Buch** *(booH)*

die **Briefmarke** *(breef-mar-kuh)*

das **Papier**

der **Kuli**

der **Bleistift** *(bly-shtift)*

der **Brief** *(breef)*

die **Brille**

die **Zeitschrift** *(tsight-shrift)*

der **Fernseher** *(fairn-zay-air)*

der **Computer** *(kohm-pyoo-tair)*

(zee) know **nun** *(noon)* how to count, how to ask **Fragen** *(frah-gen)*, how to use **Verben mit** the "plug-in" formula

und how to describe something, be it the location of a **Hotel oder die Farbe** *(far-buh)* of a **Haus**. Let's

take the basics that **Sie haben** learned **und** expand them in special areas that will be most

helpful in your travels. What does everyone do on a holiday? Send **Postkarten** of course. Let's

learn exactly how **das deutsche Postamt** *(post-ahmt)* works.
post office

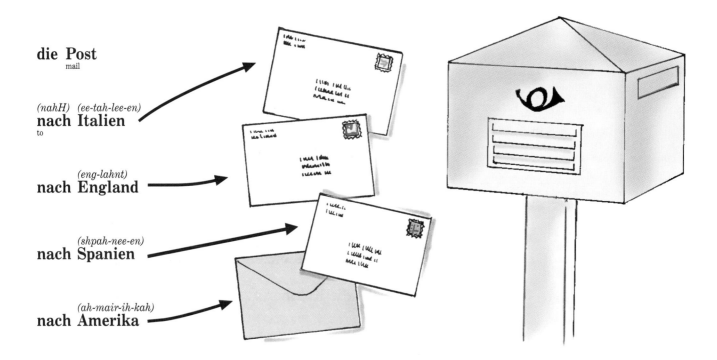

die Post
mail

(nahH) (ee-tah-lee-en)
nach Italien
to

(eng-lahnt)
nach England

(shpah-nee-en)
nach Spanien

(ah-mair-ih-kah)
nach Amerika

Das deutsche Postamt *(post-ahmt)* **ist** where **Sie** buy **Briefmarken und** send **Briefe und Postkarten. Sie**
post office
can send **Faxe** *(fahk-suh)* or make **ein Ferngespräch** *(fairn-geh-shprayH)* **von dem Postamt.** In large cities, **das Postamt**
faxes   long-distance call
hat einen Schalter *(haht) (shahl-tair)* which is **auf** abends **und am Samstag.**
counter   open   evenings

❏ **das Schweden** *(shvay-den)* . . . . Sweden
  — **wo sie Schwedisch sprechen** *(shvay-dish)*
❏ **die Schweiz** *(shvites)* . . . . Switzerland   **S**
  — **wo sie Deutsch, Italienisch und Französisch sprechen**
❏ **schwimmen** *(shvim-men)* . . . . to swim

Hier sind the necessary **Wörter für das** *(post-ahmt)* **Postamt.** Practice them aloud **und** write them in the
post office

blanks.

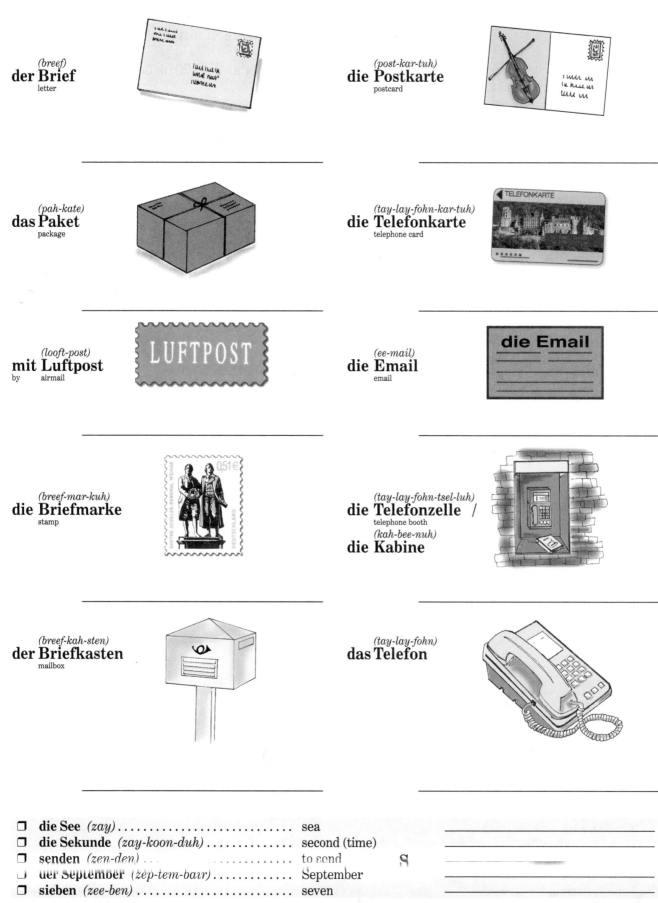

(breef)
der Brief
letter

_____

(pah-kate)
das Paket
package

_____

(looft-post)
mit Luftpost
by   airmail

_____

(breef-mar-kuh)
die Briefmarke
stamp

_____

(breef-kah-sten)
der Briefkasten
mailbox

_____

(post-kar-tuh)
die Postkarte
postcard

_____

(tay-lay-fohn-kar-tuh)
die Telefonkarte
telephone card

_____

(ee-mail)
die Email
email

_____

(tay-lay-fohn-tsel-luh)
die Telefonzelle /
telephone booth
(kah-bee-nuh)
die Kabine

_____

(tay-lay-fohn)
das Telefon

_____

_____
_____
_____
_____

Next step — **Sie** ask **Fragen** *(frah-gen)* like those **unten,** depending on **was Sie möchten.** Repeat these
would like

sentences aloud many times.

(voh) (kow-fuh)
Wo kaufe ich Briefmarken? _____
do I buy

Wo kaufe ich eine Postkarte? _____

(mah-Huh)   *(tay-lay-fohn-ahn-roof)*
Wo mache ich einen Telefonanruf? _____
do I make   telephone call

(dair) (breef-kah-sten)
Wo ist der Briefkasten? _____

(tay-lay-fohn-tsel-luh)
Wo ist die Telefonzelle? _____

(shick-uh)   *(pah-kate)*
Wo schicke ich ein Paket? _____
do I send

(gipt)   *(tay-lay-fohn-tsel-luh)*
Wo gibt es eine Telefonzelle? _____
is there

(vee) (feel)
Wie viel kostet das? _____ *Wie viel kostet das?   Wie viel kostet das?* _____

(yets-t)
Jetzt, quiz yourself. See if **Sie** can translate the following thoughts into **Deutsch.**

1. Where is the telephone booth? _____

2. Where do I make a telephone call? _____

3. Where do I buy a postcard? _____

4. Where is the post office? _____

5. Where do I buy stamps? _____

6. How much is it? _____

7. Where do I send a package? _____

8. By airmail, please. _____

ANTWORTEN

8.	Mit Luftpost, bitte.	4.	Wo ist das Postamt?
7.	Wo schicke ich ein Paket?	3.	Wo kaufe ich eine Postkarte?
6.	Wie viel kostet das?	2.	Wo mache ich einen Telefonanruf?
5.	Wo kaufe ich Briefmarken?	1.	Wo ist die Telefonzelle?

Hier sind mehr Verben.

(mah-Hen)
machen _____
to make, to do

(shry-ben)
schreiben _____
to write

(tsy-gen)
zeigen _____
to show

(beh-tsah-len)
bezahlen _____
to pay

Practice these verbs by not only filling in the blanks, but by saying them aloud many, many

times until you are comfortable with the sounds **und** the words.

(mah-Hen)
machen
to make, to do

(ahn-roof)
Ich _____ einen **Anruf.**
call

Er
Sie _____ einen **Anruf.**
Es

Wir _____ **viel.**

Sie _____ nicht **viel.**

(ahl-les)
Sie _____ **alles.**
they   everything

(shry-ben)
schreiben
to write

Ich _____ einen **Brief.**

Er
Sie *schreibt /* _____ die **Anschrift.**
Es   address *(ahn-schrift)*

Wir _____ **viel.**

(neeH-ts)
Sie _____ **nichts.**
you   nothing

Sie _____ ein **Fax.**

(tsy-gen)
zeigen
to show

(ee-nen)
Ich _____ **Ihnen** das **Buch.**
to you

Er
Sie _____ **Ihnen** das **Postamt.**
Es   to you

(shlohss)
Wir _____ **Ihnen** das **Schloss.**
castle
(post-ahmt)
Sie _____ **mir** das **Postamt.**
you   to me

(shtrah-suh)
Sie *zeigen /* _____ **mir** die **Straße.**
to me   street

(beh-tsah-len)
bezahlen
to pay (for)

(rehH-noong)
Ich _____ die **Rechnung.**
bill

Er
Sie _____ die **Karten.**
Es   tickets

(tsook-kar-ten)
Wir _____ die **Zugkarten.**
train tickets
(price)
Sie _____ den **Preis.**
price

(kohn-tsairt-kar-ten)
Sie _____ die **Konzertkarten.**
they   concert tickets

❏ **singen** *(zing-en)* . . . . to sing _____
❏ **sitzen** *(zit-tsen)* . . . . to sit
❏ **der Ski** *(she)* . . . . ski **S** _____
❏ **die Socken** *(zoh-Hen)* . . . . socks
❏ **der Sommer** *(zoh-mair)* . . . . summer _____

66

Some of these signs you probably recognize, but take a couple of minutes to review them anyway.

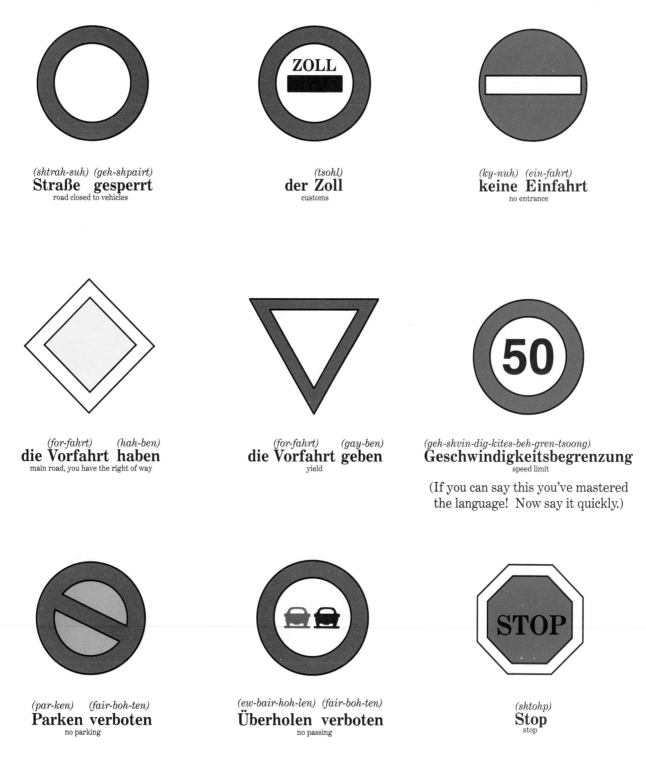

(shtrah-suh) (geh-shpairt)
Straße gesperrt
road closed to vehicles

(tsohl)
der Zoll
customs

(ky-nuh) (ein-fahrt)
keine Einfahrt
no entrance

(for-fahrt)   (hah-ben)
die Vorfahrt haben
main road, you have the right of way

(for-fahrt)   (gay-ben)
die Vorfahrt geben
yield

(geh-shvin-dig-kites-beh-gren-tsoong)
Geschwindigkeitsbegrenzung
speed limit

(If you can say this you've mastered
the language! Now say it quickly.)

(par-ken)   (fair-boh-ten)
Parken verboten
no parking

(ew-bair-hoh-len) (fair-boh-ten)
Überholen verboten
no passing

(shtohp)
Stop
stop

(oom-lie-toong)
UMLEITUNG
detour

What follows are approximate conversions, so when you order something by liters, kilograms or grams you will have an idea of what to expect and not find yourself being handed one piece of candy when you thought you ordered an entire bag.

To Convert		Do the Math		
liters (l) to gallons,	multiply by 0.26	4 liters x 0.26	=	1.04 gallons
gallons to liters,	multiply by 3.79	10 gal. x 3.79	=	37.9 liters
kilograms (kg) to pounds,	multiply by 2.2	2 kilograms x 2.2	=	4.4 pounds
pounds to kilos,	multiply by 0.46	10 pounds x 0.46	=	4.6 kg
grams (g) to ounces,	multiply by 0.035	100 grams x 0.035	=	3.5 oz.
ounces to grams,	multiply by 28.35	10 oz. x 28.35	=	283.5 g.
meters (m) to feet,	multiply by 3.28	2 meters x 3.28	=	6.56 feet
feet to meters,	multiply by 0.3	6 feet x 0.3	=	1.8 meters

For fun, take your weight in pounds and convert it into kilograms. It sounds better that way, doesn't it? How many kilometers is it from your home to school, to work, to the post office?

The Simple Versions		
one liter	=	approximately one US quart
four liters	=	approximately one US gallon
one kilo	=	approximately 2.2 pounds
100 grams	=	approximately 3.5 ounces
500 grams	=	slightly more than one pound
one meter	=	slightly more than three feet

The distance between **New York und Frankfurt** is approximately 3,844 miles. How many kilometers would that be? It is only 790 miles between **London und Wien**. How many kilometers is that?

kilometers (km.) to miles,	multiply by 0.62	1000 km. x 0.62	=	620 miles
miles to kilometers,	multiply by 1.6	1000 miles x 1.6	=	1,600 km.

Inches	1	2	3	4	5	6	7

To convert centimeters into inches, multiply by 0.39   Example: 9 cm. x 0.39   = 3.51 in.

To convert inches into centimeters, multiply by 2.54   Example: 4 in. x 2.54   = 10.16 cm.

cm 1	2	3	4	5	6	7	8	9	10	11	12	13	14	15	16	17	18

18   *(dee)* *(rehH-noong)* Die Rechnung
bill

Ja, es gibt auch bills to pay in Deutschland. Sie haben just finished your Abendessen und *(gipt)* *there are* *also* *(ah-bent-ess-en)* *evening meal*

Sie möchten die Rechnung. Was machen Sie? Sie call for den Kellner (Herr Ober!) oder die *(rehH-noong)* *(vahs)* *(mah-Hen)* *(kel-nair)* *(oh-bair)* *would like* *bill* *do you do* *waiter*

Kellnerin (Fräulein!). Der Kellner will normally reel off what Sie haben eaten while writing *(kel-nair-in)* *waitress*

rapidly. Er will then place ein Stück Papier auf den Tisch, und say „Das macht vierzig *(shtewk)* *(owf)* *(mahHt)* *makes*

Euro." Sie will pay the waiter oder perhaps Sie will pay an der Kasse. *(kah-suh)* *cashier*

Being a seasoned traveler, Sie know that tipping as Sie may know it in Amerika ist nicht the

the same in Deutschland. Generally, die Bedienung ist included in den Preisen. When the *(beh-dee-noong)* *(pry-zen)* *service* *prices*

service is not included in the Rechnung, round the bill up oder simply leave what you consider *bill*

an appropriate amount for your Kellner auf dem Tisch. When Sie dine out on your Reise, it *(ry-zuh)* *trip*

may be a good idea to make a reservation. It can be difficult to get into a popular Restaurant.

Nevertheless, the experience is well worth the trouble Sie might encounter to obtain a reservation.

Und remember, Sie know enough Deutsch to make a reservation. Just speak slowly and clearly.

❏ die Sonne *(zoh-nuh)* . . . . sun
❏ die Spezialität *(shpay-tsee-ah-lih-tate)* . . . . . . specialty
❏ das Spanien *(shpah-nee-en)* . . . . Spain   **S**
    — wo sie Spanisch sprechen *(shpah-nish)*
❏ der Sport *(shport)* . . . . sport

Remember these key **Wörter** when dining out in **Deutschland,** *(ur-stair-ry-sh)* **Österreich oder in der Schweiz.**
Austria   Switzerland

(kel-nair)
der Kellner _____
waiter

(kel-nair-in)
die Kellnerin _____
waitress

(rehH-noong)
die Rechnung ___ die Rechnung ___
bill

(trink-gelt)
das Trinkgeld _____
tip

(shpy-zuh-kar-tuh)
die Speisekarte _____
menu

(kvih-toong)
die Quittung _____
receipt

(ent-shool-dee-goong)
Entschuldigung _____
excuse me

(dahn-kuh)
danke _____
thank you

(bit-tuh)
bitte _____
please

(gay-ben) (zee) (mir)
Geben Sie mir . . . _____
give   me

(kohn-vair-zah-tsee-ohn)
Hier ist a sample **Konversation** involving paying **die Rechnung** when leaving a **Hotel.**
(rehH-noong)
bill

(yoh-hah-nes)
Johannes:

(ent-shool-dee-goong) *(rehH-noong)* *(beh-tsah-len)*
Entschuldigung. Ich möchte die Rechnung bezahlen.

___ *Entschuldigung. Ich möchte die Rechnung bezahlen.* ___

Hotelmanager:

(vel-Hes)
Welches Zimmer, bitte?
which   room

_____

Johannes:

Zimmer dreihundertzehn.

_____

Hotelmanager:

(eye-nen)
Danke. Einen Moment, bitte.

_____

Hotelmanager:

(rehH-noong)
Hier ist die Rechnung.

_____

(pro-blame-uh)
If **Sie** have any **Probleme mit den Nummern,** just ask someone to write out **die Nummern** so

Sie can be sure you understand everything correctly,

(shry-ben) *(owf)*
„**Bitte, schreiben Sie die Nummern auf! Danke.**"
please   write out

Practice: _____
(Please write out the numbers. Thank you.)

- ❒ **der Staat** *(shtaht)* . . . . state, country _____
- ❒ **der Student** *(shtoo-dent)* . . . . student (male) _____
- ❒ **die Studentin** *(shtoo-dent-in)* . . . . student (female) **S** _____
- ❒ **der Sturm** *(shturm)* . . . . storm _____
- ❒ **das Südamerika** *(zewt-ah-mair-ih-kah)* . . . . . . South America

Nun, let's take a break from **die Rechnungen** *(rehH-noong-en)* **und das Geld** *(gelt)* **und** learn some fun, **neue** *(noy-uh)* **Wörter.**

bills ⸱ money ⸱ new

Sie can always practice these **Wörter** by using your flash cards at the back of this **Buch.** Carry these flash cards in your purse, pocket, briefcase **oder** knapsack **und** *use them!*

(owf)
auf
open

_____

(tsoo)
zu
closed

_____

(grohs)
groß
big / tall

_____

(kline)
klein
small / short

_____

(geh-zoont)
gesund
healthy

_____

(krahnk)
krank
sick

_____

(goot)
gut
good

_____

(shlehHt)
schlecht
bad

_____

(hice)
heiß
hot

_____

(kahlt)
kalt
cold

_____

❑ **die Suppe** *(zoo-puh)* . . . . soup
❑ **die Symphonie** *(zoom-foh-nee)* . . . . symphony
In the following **Wörter,** notice how often the initial „**T**" becomes a "D" in English.
❑ **der Tag** *(tahk)* . . . . day
❑ **der Tanz** *(tahn-ts)* . . . . dance

s _____

t _____

71

(koorts)
kurz _____
short

(lahng)
lang _____
long

(lahng-zahm)
langsam _____
slow

(shnel)
schnell _____
fast

(ahlt)
alt _____
old

(yoong)
jung _____
young

(hohH)
hoch _____
high

(nee-drig)
niedrig _____
low

(toy-air)
teuer _____
expensive

(bil-lig)
billig _____
inexpensive

(ry-sh)
reich _____
rich

(arm)
arm _____
poor

(feel)
viel _____
a lot

(vay-nig)
wenig _____
a little

❐ **tanzen** *(tahn-tsen)* . . . . to dance _____
❐ **die Tochter** *(tohH-tair)* . . . . daughter _____
❐ **träumen** *(troy-men)* . . . . to dream _____
❐ **tun** *(toon)* . . . . to do _____
❐ **die Tür** *(tewr)* . . . . door _____

(noy-en)
Hier sind die neuen Verben.

(viss-en)
wissen _____
to know (fact)

(kur-nen)
können _____
to be able to, can

(lay-zen)
lesen _____
to read

(mew-sen)
müssen _____
to have to, must

Study the patterns below closely, as **Sie** will use these verbs a lot.

(viss-en)
wissen
to know

Adenauerstr. 15

Ich _weiß /_ _____ alles. *(ahl-les)* everything

Er
Sie _weiß /_ _____, wann der Zug kommt. *(tsook)* train comes
Es

Wir _wissen /_ _____, wie alt er ist. *(vee)* *(air)*

Sie _____, wo das Hotel ist. *(voh)*
you

Sie _____ nichts. *(neeH-ts)*

(kur-nen)
können
to be able to, can

Ich kann
Deutsch
sprechen.

Ich _kann /_ _____ Deutsch sprechen. *(shpreh-Hen)*

Er
Sie _kann /_ _____ Deutsch lesen. *(lay-zen)* read
Es

Wir _können /_ _____ Englisch sprechen.

Sie _____ Deutsch verstehen. *(fair-shtay-en)*

Sie _____ Italienisch sprechen. *(ee-tah-lee-ay-nish)*
they

(lay-zen)
lesen
to read

Ich _lese /_ _____ das Buch. *(booH)*

Er
Sie _liest /_ _____ die Zeitschrift. *(tsight-shrift)* magazine
Es

Wir _lesen /_ _____ wenig. *(vay-nig)*

Sie _____ viel. *(feel)* a lot

Sie _____ die Zeitung. *(voh)* newspaper
they

(mew-sen)
müssen
to have to, must

Ich _muss /_ _____ Deutsch lernen. *(lair-nen)*

Er
Sie _muss /_ _____ das Buch lesen. *(lay-zen)*
Es

Wir _müssen /_ _____ das Schloss sehen. *(shlohss)* castle *(zay-en)*

Sie _____ einen Brief schreiben. *(shry-ben)*
you

Sie _____ die Rechnung bezahlen. *(rehH-noong)*

❏ **die Uniform** *(oo-nee-form)* . . . . uniform
❏ **das Ungarn** *(oon-garn)* . . . . Hungary
 — **wo sie Ungarisch sprechen** *(oon-gar-ish)*
❏ **uninteressant** *(oon-in-tair-es-sahnt)* . . . . uninteresting
❏ **die Universität** *(oo-nih-vair-zih-tate)* . . . . . . university

u

_____

_____

_____

_____

Notice that **"können" und "müssen"** along with **"möchte"** and **"möchten"** can be combined

with another verb. **"Wissen"** is a bit different **aber** (ah-bair) **sehr wichtig.**
but

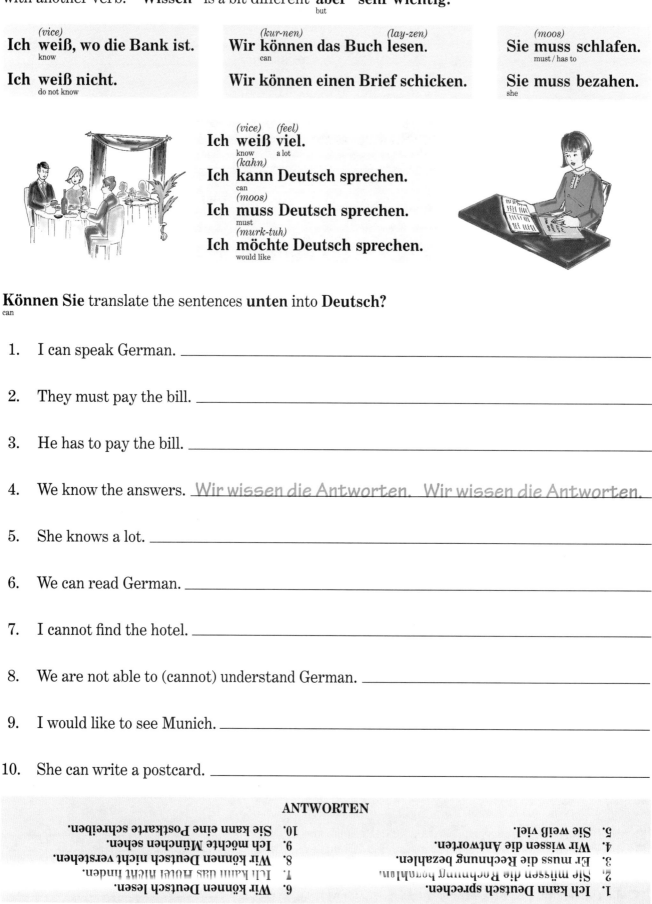

Ich weiß, wo die Bank ist.
(vice)
know

Ich weiß nicht.
do not know

Wir können das Buch lesen.
(kur-nen) (lay-zen)
can

Wir können einen Brief schicken.

Sie muss schlafen.
(moos)
must / has to

Sie muss bezahen.
she

Ich weiß viel.
(vice) (feel)
know a lot

Ich kann Deutsch sprechen.
(kahn)
can

Ich muss Deutsch sprechen.
(moos)
must

Ich möchte Deutsch sprechen.
(murk-tuh)
would like

Können Sie translate the sentences **unten** into **Deutsch?**
can

1. I can speak German. _____

2. They must pay the bill. _____

3. He has to pay the bill. _____

4. We know the answers. *Wir wissen die Antworten.   Wir wissen die Antworten.*

5. She knows a lot. _____

6. We can read German. _____

7. I cannot find the hotel. _____

8. We are not able to (cannot) understand German. _____

9. I would like to see Munich. _____

10. She can write a postcard. _____

74

Jetzt, draw **Linien** between the opposites **unten.** Do not forget to say them out loud. Say these

lines

Wörter every day to describe **Dinge in Ihrem Haus, in der Schule oder** at work.

(ear-em) *your*   *(dair)* *(shoo-luh)*
home   *school*

(grohs)
groß

(oh-ben)
oben

links

(owf)
auf

(yoong)
jung

(koorts)
kurz

arm

billig

(krahnk)
krank

(vay-nig)
wenig

(lahng)
lang

(geh-zoont)
gesund

(feel)
viel

schnell

(goot)
gut

(ahlt)
alt

(hice)
heiß

klein

(oon-ten)
unten

(rehH-ts)
rechts

(lahng-zahm)
langsam

(kahlt)
kalt

(toy-air)
teuer

(ry-sh)
reich

(tsoo)
zu

(shlehHt)
schlecht

❏ **der Untergrund** *(oon-tair-groont)* . . . . underground, subway
❏ **unten** *(oon-ten)* . . . . downstairs   **u**
❏ **unter** *(oon-tair)* . . . . under
❏ **unterwegs** *(oon-tair-vehgs)* . . . . in transit, on the way
❏ **die Unterwelt** *(oon-tair-velt)* . . . . underworld

(ry-zen) *(ry-zen)* *(ry-zen)*

Reisen, Reisen, Reisen
to travel

(mewn-shen)
Gestern nach München!
yesterday

(hahm-boorg)
Heute nach Hamburg!
today

(bair-leen)
Morgen nach Berlin!
tomorrow

If you know a few key **Wörter,** traveling can be very easy in German-speaking countries.

(zair) *(grohs)*
Deutschland ist nicht sehr groß, in fact, it is approximately *(zoh)* **so groß** *(vee)* **wie Oregon und**
large   as   as

(tsoo-zah-men)
Washington zusammen. Das macht das Reisen sehr einfach. Wie reisen Sie?
together   *(ry-zen)*   *(ein-fahH)* *(vee)* *(ry-zen)*
                                                                        simple, easy

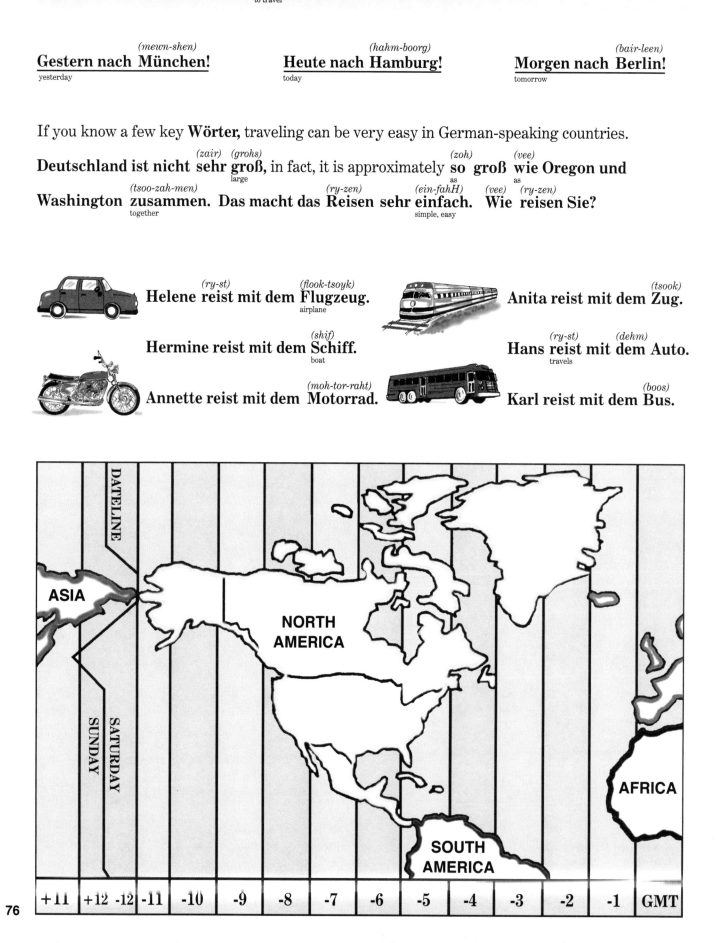

(ry-st)   *(flook-tsoyk)*
Helene reist mit dem Flugzeug.
airplane

(tsook)
Anita reist mit dem Zug.

(shif)
Hermine reist mit dem Schiff.
boat

(ry-st)   *(dehm)*
Hans reist mit dem Auto.
travels

(moh-tor-raht)
Annette reist mit dem Motorrad.

(boos)
Karl reist mit dem Bus.

ASIA			NORTH AMERICA								AFRICA		

DATELINE

SATURDAY SUNDAY

SOUTH AMERICA

+11	+12	-12	-11	-10	-9	-8	-7	-6	-5	-4	-3	-2	-1	GMT

When **Sie** are traveling, **Sie** will want to tell others your nationality **und Sie** will meet people from all corners of the world. Can you guess where someone is from if they say one of the following? **Die Antworten** are in your glossary beginning on page 108.

Ich komme aus England. *(ows)* *(eng-lahnt)* _____
come   from

Ich komme aus Italien. *(ee-tah-lee-en)* _____
come   from

Ich komme aus Frankreich. *(frahnk-ry-sh)* _____
from

Ich komme aus Spanien. *(shpah-nee-en)* _____

Ich komme aus Belgien. *(bel-gee-en)* _____

Ich komme aus der Schweiz. *(dair) (shvites)* _____

Ich komme aus Polen. *(poh-len)* _____

Ich komme aus Dänemark. *(day-nuh-mark)* _____

Ich komme aus Österreich. *(ur-stair-ry-sh)* _____

Wir kommen aus Norwegen. *(nor-vay-gen)* _____
we   come

Wir kommen aus Schweden. *(shvay-den)* _____
we   come

Wir kommen aus der Slowakei. *(sloh-vah-kai)* _____

Wir kommen aus Ungarn. *(oon-garn)* _____

Er kommt aus Holland. *(hohl-lahnt)* _____
he comes

Er kommt aus Kroatien. *(kroh-aht-zee-en)* _____

Sie kommt aus Russland. *(roos-lahnt)* _____
she comes

Sie kommt aus Südafrika. *(zewt-ah-frih-kah)* _____

Ich komme aus Kanada. *(kah-nah-dah)* _____

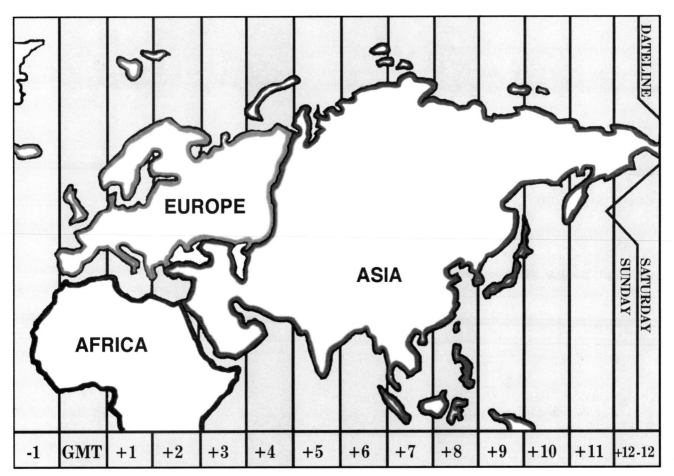

(doy-chen)
Die Deutschen love to travel, so **es ist** no surprise to find many **Wörter** built on the **Wort**
(ry-zen)
„**Reisen**" which can mean either "trip" **oder** "to travel." Practice saying the following **Wörter**

(ohft)
many times. **Sie** will see them **oft.**
often

(ry-zen)
reisen _____
to travel

(ry-zuh-bew-roh)
das Reisebüro _____
travel agency

(ry-zen-duh)
der Reisende _____
traveler

(goo-tuh) (ry-zuh)
Gute Reise! _____
have a good trip

If **Sie** choose to travel **mit dem Auto,** here are a few key **Wörter.**

(ow-toh-bahn)
die Autobahn _____
freeway

(ein-fahrt)
die Einfahrt _____
entrance for a vehicle

(shtrah-suh)
die Straße _____
street, road

(ows-fahrt)
die Ausfahrt _____
exit for a vehicle

(meet-vah-gen)
der Mietwagen _____
rental car

(tahnk-shtel-luh)
die Tankstelle _____
service station

(gahng)
Unten sind some basic signs which **Sie** should **auch** learn to recognize quickly. **Gang** comes from

(dee-zen)
the verb **gehen** meaning "to go" **oder** "to walk." That should help you **mit diesen Wörtern.**
these

EINGANG

AUSGANG

(ein-gahng)
der Eingang _____
entrance

(ows-gahng)
der Ausgang _____
exit

(howpt-ein-gahng)
der Haupteingang _____
main entrance

(noht-ows-gahng)
der Notausgang _____
emergency exit

DRÜCKEN

ZIEHEN

(drew-ken)
drücken _____
to push (doors)

(tsee-en)
ziehen _____
to pull (doors)

❒ **der Vater** *(fah-tair)* . . . . father _____
    — **Der Vater heißt Herr Taler.**
❒ **voll** *(fohl)* . . . . full **v** _____
    Das Glas ist voll.
    — **Der Mann ist voll.** (drunk)

78

Let's learn the basic travel verbs. Take out a piece of paper **und** make up your own sentences

with these **neuen Wörtern.** _(noy-en)_ _(vur-tairn)_ Follow the same pattern **Sie haben** in previous Steps.

(flee-gen)
fliegen _____
to fly

(zit-tsen)
sitzen _____
to sit

(ahn-koh-men)
ankommen _____
to arrive

(fah-ren)
fahren _____
to drive, to travel by vehicle

(ahp-fah-ren)
abfahren _____
to leave, depart

(pah-ken)
packen _____
to pack

(gipt)
es gibt _____
there is, there are

(oom-shty-gen)
umsteigen _____
to transfer (vehicles)

Hier sind mehr neue Wörter für die Reise.

(flook-hah-fen)
der Flughafen
airport

(bahn-shtaig)
der Bahnsteig
platform

_____

_____

(far-plahn)
der Fahrplan
timetable

Von Berlin nach Leipzig		
Abfahrt	**Zug Nr.**	**Ankunft**
04:13	567	06:13
09:42	1433	11:45
12:40	1892	15:00
15:10	32	17:30
19:19	650	21:50

(bahn-hohf)
der Bahnhof
train station

_____

_____

❏ **die Vereinigten Staaten** _(fair-eye-neeg-ten)(shtah-ten)_ United States _____
— **Ich wohne in den Vereinigten Staaten.**
— **Ich komme aus den Vereinigten Staaten.** **V** _____
❏ **das Volk** _(folk)_ .... folk, people _____
— **das deutsche Volk**

79

Mit *(dee-zen)* **diesen Wörtern, Sie sind** ready for any **Reise**, anywhere. **Sie** should have no **Probleme**
these

mit these new verbs, just remember the basic "plug-in" formula **Sie haben** already learned. Use

that knowledge to translate the following thoughts into **Deutsch. Die Antworten sind unten.**

1. I fly to Berlin. _____

2. I drive to Bonn. _____

3. He travels by (with the) train to Heidelberg. _____

4. We sit in the airplane. _____

5. We buy three tickets to Frankfurt. _____

6. They travel to Salzburg. _____

7. Where is the train to Vienna? _____

8. How do we fly to Germany? With Lufthansa? _____

_____

Hier sind some **wichtige Wörter für** *(ry-zen-duh)* **Reisende.**
travelers

Von Innsbruck nach München		
Abfahrt	**Zug Nr.**	**Ankunft**
08:32	118	11:46
11:35	413	14:52
14:11	718	17:52
18:12	1132	22:53
Gute Reise!		

(beh-zets-t)
besetzt _____
occupied

(ahp-fahrt)
die Abfahrt _____
departure

(fry)
frei _____
free

(ahn-koonft)
die Ankunft _____
arrival

(ahp-tile)
das Abteil _____
compartment, wagon

(ows-lahnt)
das Ausland _____
foreign country

(plahts)
der Platz _____
seat

(in-lahnt)
das Inland _____
domestic, internal (of the country)

ANTWORTEN

1. **Ich fliege nach Berlin.**
2. **Ich fahre nach Bonn.**
3. **Er fährt mit dem Zug nach Heidelberg.**
3. **Er reist mit dem Zug nach Heidelberg.**
4. **Wir sitzen in dem Flugzeug.**

5. **Wir kaufen drei Karten nach Frankfurt.**
6. **Sie reisen nach Salzburg.**
7. **Wo ist der Zug nach Wien?**
8. **Wie fliegen wir nach Deutschland? Mit Lufthansa?**

Increase your travel **Wörter** by writing out **die Wörter unten und** practicing the sample

sentences out loud. Practice asking *(frah-gen)* **Fragen mit „wo.“** It will help you later.

(nahH)
nach _____
to   **Wo ist der Zug nach Dresden?**

(glice)
das Gleis _____
track   **Wo ist Gleis Nummer sieben?**

(foont-bew-roh)
das Fundbüro _____
lost-and-found office   **Gibt es ein Fundbüro?**

(bahn-shtaig)
der Bahnsteig _____
platform   **Wo ist Bahnsteig fünf-A?**

(flook)
der Flug _____
flight   **Wo ist der Flug nach Innsbruck?**

(plahts)
der Platz _____
seat   **Ist dieser Platz frei?**

(veck-zel-shtoo-buh)
die Wechselstube _____
money-exchange office   **Gibt es eine Wechselstube?**

(shahl-tair)
der Schalter _____
counter   **Wo ist Schalter Nummer acht?**

(var-tuh-zahl)
der Wartesaal _____
waiting room   **Gibt es einen Wartesaal?**

(shpy-zuh-vah-gen)
der Speisewagen _____
dining car   **Gibt es einen Speisewagen?**

(shlahf-vah-gen)
der Schlafwagen _____
sleeping car   **Gibt es einen Schlafwagen?**

(lee-guh-vah-gen)
der Liegewagen _____
car with berths   **Wo ist der Liegewagen?**

_____ _____ **kommt der Zug an?**   _____ _____ **ist los?**
(when)   (when)   *(tsook)* arrives   (what)   (what)   *(lohs)*

❐ **von** *(fohn)* . . . . from   _____
   — **Die Frau kommt von Frankfurt.**   **v**
❐ **vor** *(for)* . . . . before, in front of   _____
❐ **der Vorname** *(for-nah-muh)* . . . . first name, given name   _____
   — **Der Vater heißt Helmut mit Vornamen.**

Können Sie the following **lesen?** *(lay-zen)*
can

← Sie sitzen nun in dem Flugzeug und Sie

fliegen *(flee-gen)* **nach Deutschland. Sie haben das**

Geld, die Fahrkarten und den Pass. *(pahss)* **Sie**
passport

sind nun Tourist. Sie landen morgen

in Deutschland. Gute Reise! Viel Spaß! *(shpahs)*

Deutsche Züge *(tsue-guh)* come in many shapes, sizes, **und** speeds. **Es gibt** *(gipt)* **Regionalbahn (RB) Züge** *(ray-gee-oh-nahl-bahn)(air-bay)(tsue-guh)*
trains   there are

(sehr langsam), RegionalExpress (RE) Züge *(ray-gee-oh-nahl-eks-press) (air-ay)* **(langsam), InterregioExpress (IRE) Züge** *(in-tair-ray-gee-oh-eks-press) (ee-air-ay)*

(schnell), und InterCity Züge (sehr schnell). If **Sie** plan to travel a long distance, **Sie** may

wish to catch an **InterCity** train or **ICE (InterCity Express)** which are the fastest **und** make the

fewest intermediate stops.

❐ **das Wasser** *(vah-sair)* .... water	
❐ **der Westen** *(ves-ten)* .... West	
❐ **das Wild** *(vilt)* .... venison, game **W**	
❐ **der Wein** *(vine)* .... wine	
❐ **der Wind** *(vint)* .... wind	

82

Knowing these travel **Wörter** will make your holiday twice as enjoyable **und** at least three times as easy. Review these **Reisewörter** by doing the crossword puzzle **unten**. Drill yourself on this Step by selecting other destinations **und** ask your own **Fragen** about **Züge, Busse, oder Flugzeuge** *(flook-tsoy-guh)* that go there. Select more **neue Wörter** from your **Wörterbuch und** ask your own **Fragen** beginning with **wann, wo und wie viel**. **Die Antworten** to the crossword puzzle are at the bottom of the next page.

ACROSS

2. yesterday
6. sleeping car
8. I
9. with
10. occupied
11. bus
12. passport
14. to pack
16. to, towards
17. and
18. to travel
22. domestic
24. to sit
25. nothing
27. exit (for people)
28. to drive, go
29. train

DOWN

1. restaurant
2. money
3. to rain
4. rental car
5. clock, time
7. airport
13. ship
15. now
19. dining car
20. track
21. train station
23. foreign country
26. place, seat

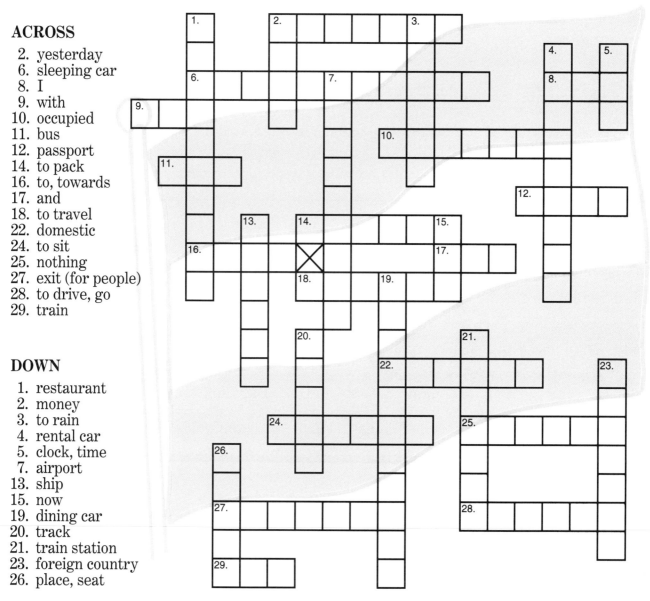

Did **Sie** recognize the flag of **Österreich**? Every year **Österreich** hosts the Salzburg Festival, a celebration of **Musik** in the birthplace of Wolfgang Amadeus Mozart.

❏ **der Winter** *(vin-tair)* . . . . winter
❏ **der Wolle** *(voh-luh)* . . . . wool
❏ **das Willkommen** *(vil-koh-men)* . . . . welcome **W**
❏ **wandern** *(vahn-dairn)* . . . . to wander, hike
❏ **die Waren** *(vah-ren)* . . . . wares, goods

What about inquiring about **Preisen?** **Sie** *(kur-nen)* **können** das *(owH)* **auch** *(frah-gen)* **fragen.**
prices   can   ask

(vahs)   *(hi-del-bairg)*
Was kostet eine Karte nach Heidelberg? _____

(veen)
Was kostet eine Karte nach Wien? _____
                                Vienna

(vahs)   *(koh-pen-hah-gen)*
Was kostet eine Karte nach Kopenhagen? _____

(ein-fahH)
einfach _____
one-way

(hin) *(oont)* *(tsoo-rewk)*
hin und zurück _____
round-trip

What about   *(ahp-fahrt)*   *(ahn-koonft)*   times? **Sie** *(kur-nen)* **können** das *(dahs)* **auch fragen.**
           Abfahrt und Ankunft
           departure   arrival

(vahn) *(fleegt)*   *(flook-tsoyk)*   *(rohm)* *(ahp)*
Wann fliegt das Flugzeug nach Rom ab? _____
departs   Rome

(fairt)   *(tsook)*   *(prahg)*
Wann fährt der Zug nach Prag ab? _____
departs   Prague

(fairt)   *(mar-boorg)*
Wann fährt der Zug nach Marburg ab? _____

(ows) *(bair-leen)* *(ahn)*
Wann kommt der Zug aus Berlin an? _____
arrives   from

(flook-tsoyk)   *(zahlts-boorg)*
Wann kommt das Flugzeug aus Salzburg an? _____
flight

Sie have just arrived **in Deutschland. Sie sind nun** *(ahm)* **am** *(bahn-hohf)* **Bahnhof. Wo** do you wish to go?
                                      at the

Nach München? Nach Nürnberg? Tell that to the person at the *(shahl-tair)* **Schalter** selling **Karten!**
                                                counter

(murk-tuh)
Ich möchte nach Innsbruck fahren. _____
                  to travel, go

(vahn) *(fairt)*   *(tsook)*
Wann fährt der Zug nach Innsbruck? _____

(vahs)
Was kostet eine Karte nach Innsbruck? _____

Now that **Sie** know the words essential for traveling **in Deutschland, Österreich oder in der** *(ur-stair-ry-sh)*
(shvites)
Schweiz, what are some specialty items **Sie** might go in search of?

(vy-nuh)
Weine
wines

(ahn-denk-en)
Andenken
souvenirs

(shoh-koh-lah-den)
Schokoladen
chocolates

(beer-shty-nuh)
Biersteine
beer mugs

(vy-nahHts-geh-shen-kuh)
Weihnachtsgeschenke
Christmas presents

(koo-kooks-oor)
die Kuckucksuhr
cuckoo clock

Consider using GERMAN *a language map*® as well. GERMAN *a language map*® is the perfect

companion for your travels when **Sie** may not wish to take along this **Buch.** Each section

focuses on essentials for your **Reise.** Your *Language Map*® is not meant to replace learning

Deutsch, but will help you in the event **Sie** forget something and need a little bit of help. For

more information about the *Language Map*® Series, please turn to page 132 or go to www.bbks.com.

❐ **warm** *(varm)* . . . . warm
❐ **die Warnung** *(var-noong)* . . . . warning
❐ **wünschen** *(vewn-shen)* . . . . to wish   **W**
  — Was wünschen Sie?
❐ **der Weg** *(veg)* . . . . way

85

20 Die Speisekarte
(shpy-zuh-kar-tuh)
menu

Sie sind nun in Deutschland und Sie haben ein Hotelzimmer. Sie haben Hunger. Wo gibt es
(hoh-tel-tsih-mair) *(hoong-air)*
is there

ein gutes Restaurant? First of all, **es gibt** different types of places to eat. Let's learn them.
(goo-tes)
there are

das Gasthaus *(gahst-house)*
_____
an inn with a full range of meals

das Café *(kah-fay)*
_____
a coffee shop with pastries, snacks **und** beverages;
this should be a regular stop every day about 3:30 p.m.

der Schnellimbiss *(shnel-im-biss)*
_____
a snack bar, specializing in **Wurst und** beverages

die Weinstube *(vine-shtoo-buh)*
_____
a small, cozy restaurant specializing in **Weine** with some hot dishes, cheeses, **und** snacks

der Ratskeller *(rahts-kel-air)*
_____
a restaurant frequently found in the basement of **das Rathaus**
city hall

If **Sie** look around you **in einem deutschen Restaurant, Sie** will see that some customs might be

different from yours. Sharing **Tische mit** others **ist** a common **und sehr** pleasant custom.
(tish-uh)
tables

Before beginning your meal, be sure to wish those sharing your table – „**Guten Appetit!**"
(goo-ten) *(ah-peh-teet)*
enjoy your meal

Your turn to practice now.

_____
(enjoy your meal)

And at least one more time for practice!

_____
(enjoy your meal)

❐ **der Zentimeter** *(tsen-tih-may-tair)*	centimeter		_____
❐ **das Zentrum** *(tsen-troom)*	center		_____
❐ **die Zeremonie** *(tsair-eh-moh-nee)*	ceremony	**Z**	_____
❐ die Zigarette *(tsih-gah-ret-tuh)*	cigarette		_____
❐ **die Zigarre** *(tsih-gah-ruh)*	cigar		_____

86

Start imagining now all the new taste treats you will experience abroad. Try all of the different

types of eating establishments mentioned on the previous page. Experiment. If **Sie finden ein**

Restaurant that **Sie möchten** to try, consider calling ahead to make a **Reservierung.**
(rez-air-veer-oong)
reservation

(rez-air-veer-en)   *(brow-Hen)*   *(shpy-zuh-kar-tuh)*
„Ich möchte einen Tisch reservieren." If **Sie brauchen eine Speisekarte,** catch the attention
reserve   need

of the **Kellner,** saying

> *(hair) (oh-bair)   (shpy-zuh-kar-tuh)*
> **Herr Ober! Die Speisekarte, bitte.**

(Waiter. The menu, please.)

If your **Kellner** asks if **Sie** enjoyed your

(ess-en)   *(dahn-kuh)*
Essen, a smile **und** a **„Ja, danke"** will tell him
meal

that you did.

(doy-chuh)   (res-toh-rahnts)   *(shpy-zuh-kar-tuh)*
Most **deutsche Restaurants** post **die Speisekarte** outside **oder** inside. Do not hesitate to ask to

(viss-en)   *(pry-zen)*
see **die Speisekarte** before being seated so **Sie wissen** what type of meals **und Preisen Sie** will
know   prices

(tah-ges-geh-reeHt)   *(men-ew)*
encounter. Most **Restaurants** offer **ein Tagesgericht oder ein Menü**. These are complete
daily special   special meal

(price)
meals at a fair **Preis.**
price

❏ **der Zirkus** *(tseer-koos)* . . . . circus   _____
❏ **die Zivilisation** *(tsih-vih-lih-zah-tsee-ohn)* . . . civilization   _____
❏ **der Zoo** *(tsoh)* . . . . zoo   **Z**   _____
❏ **zu** *(tsoo)* . . . . to, too   _____
❏ **der Zucker** *(tsoo-kair)* . . . . sugar   _____

In Deutschland gibt es drei main meals to enjoy every day, plus perhaps **Kaffee und Kuchen**
(kah-fay) *(koo-Hen)*
there are   cake

(fewr)   *(shpay-ten)*
für the tired traveler in the **späten Nachmittag.**
                                                                                    late

(frew-shtewk)
das Frühstück _____
breakfast

In Hotels und Pensionen this meal may start as early as 6:00 and finish at 8:00.
(pahn-see-oh-nen)
guest houses

Check serving times before **Sie** retire for the night or you might miss out!

(mit-tahk-ess-en)
das Mittagessen _____
mid-day meal, lunch

generally served from 11:30 to 14:00; you will be able to find any type of meal, **groß**

oder klein, served at this time. For most people, this **ist** the main meal of the day.

(ah-bent-ess-en)
das Abendessen _____
evening meal, dinner

generally served from 18:00 to 20:30 and sometimes later; frequently after 21:30,
(hi-suh)
only cold snacks **oder heiße Wurst** are served in **Restaurants**

Nun for a preview of delights to come . . . At the back of this **Buch, Sie** will find a sample

deutsche Speisekarte. Lesen Sie die Speisekarte heute und lernen Sie die neuen Wörter.
                                      (lay-zen)   *(hoy-tuh)*   *(lair-nen)*
                                      read   today   learn

When **Sie** are ready to leave on your **Reise,** cut out **die Speisekarte,** fold it, **und** carry it in your

pocket, wallet **oder** purse. Before you go, how do **Sie** say these **drei** phrases which are so very

important for the hungry traveler?

Excuse me. I would like to reserve a table. _____

Waiter! The menu, please. _____

Enjoy your meal! _____

_____ **isst Gulasch?**   _____ **trinkt Tee?**
(who)   *(isst) (goo-lahsh)*   (who)   *(tay)*
                eats   drinks

_____ (who)

_____ **reist nach Salzburg?**
              (ry-st)   *(zahlts-boorg)*
(who)

Learning the following should help you to identify what **Sie** have ordered **und wie** it will be prepared.
- [ ] **vom Rind** *(fohm)(rint)* . . . . beef _____
- [ ] **vom Kalb** *(kahlp)* . . . . veal _____
- [ ] ~~vom Schwein~~ *(shvyn)* . . . . pork
- [ ] **vom Lamm** *(lahm)* . . . . lamb _____

Die Speisekarte unten hat the main categories **Sie** will find in most restaurants. Learn them **heute** so that **Sie** will easily recognize them when you dine **in Berlin oder in Wien.** *(bair-leen)* Berlin *(veen)* Vienna. Be sure to write the words in the blanks below.

(shpy-zuh-kar-tuh)
die Speisekarte

(for-shpy-zen)
Vorspeisen
appetizers

(zoo-pen)
Suppen
soups

(eye-air-shpy-zen)
Eierspeisen
egg dishes

(fish-geh-reeH-tuh)
Fischgerichte
fish dishes

(howpt-geh-reeH-tuh)
Hauptgerichte
entrees, main meals

(fahn-en-geh-reeH-tuh)
Grill- und Pfannengerichte
grilled and pan-fried food

(geh-mew-zuh)
Gemüse
vegetables

(zah-lah-tuh)
Salate
salads

(nahH-tish)
Nachtisch
dessert

(kahl-tuh) (shpy-zen)
Kalte Speisen
cold meals (plates of cheese and cold cuts)

(ice)
Eis
ice cream

(koo-Hen)
Kuchen
pastries, cake

(geh-trenk-uh)
Getränke
beverages

❐ **der Hammel** *(hah-mel)*	sheep	_____
❐ **das Geflügel** *(geh-flew-gel)*	poultry	_____
❐ **das Wild** *(wilt)*	game	_____
❐ **gebraten** *(geh-brah-ten)*	roasted, fried	_____
❐ **im Backteig** *(bahk-taig)*	in batter	_____

89

Sie may also order **Gemüse** *(geh-mew-zuh)* und **Kartoffeln** *(kar-toh-feln)* mit your **Essen und einen gemischten** *(geh-mish-ten)* **Salat.** *(zah-laht)*

One day at an open-air **Markt** will teach you **die Namen** *(nah-men)* for all the different kinds of **Gemüse** *(geh-mew-zuh)* und **Obst,** *(ohpst)* plus it will be a delightful experience for you. **Sie können** *(kur-nen)* always consult your menu guide at the back of this **Buch** if **Sie** forget **die richtigen Namen. Nun** *(noon)* **Sie** *(zee)* are seated, **und der Kellner kommt.**

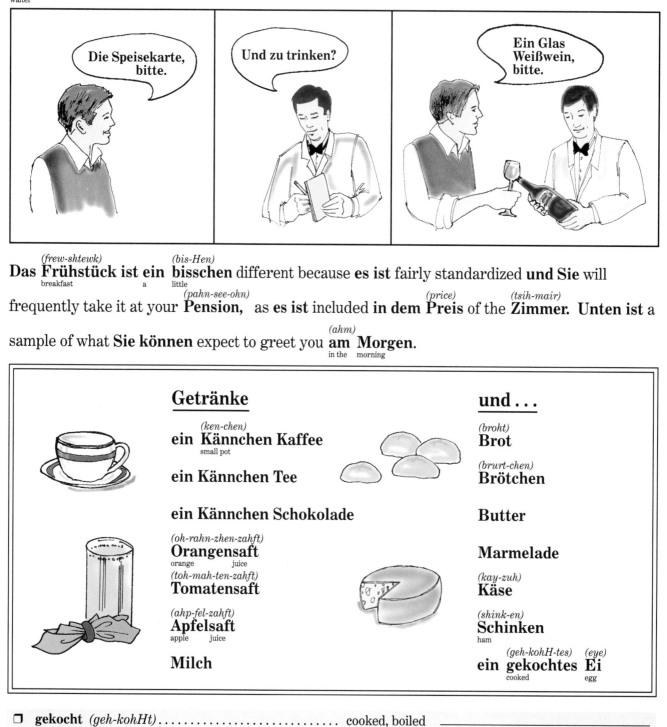

Die Speisekarte, bitte.

Und zu trinken?

Ein Glas Weißwein, bitte.

Das Frühstück ist ein *(frew-shtewk)* **bisschen** *(bis-Hen)* different because **es ist** fairly standardized **und Sie** will frequently take it at your **Pension,** *(pahn-see-ohn)* as **es ist** included **in dem Preis** *(price)* of the **Zimmer.** *(tsih-mair)* **Unten ist** a sample of what **Sie können** expect to greet you **am Morgen.** *(ahm)* / in the morning

Getränke   und . . .

ein **Kännchen Kaffee** *(ken-chen)* / small pot

ein **Kännchen Tee**

ein **Kännchen Schokolade**

Orangensaft *(oh-rahn-zhen-zahft)* / orange juice

Tomatensaft *(toh-mah-ten-zahft)*

Apfelsaft *(ahp-fel-zahft)* / apple juice

Milch

Brot *(broht)*

Brötchen *(brurt-chen)*

Butter

Marmelade

Käse *(kay-zuh)*

Schinken *(shink-en)* / ham

ein **gekochtes Ei** *(geh-kohH-tes)* *(eye)* / cooked egg

□ **gekocht** *(geh-kohHt)* . . . . cooked, boiled _____
□ **gebacken** *(geh-bah-ken)* . . . . baked _____
□ **gegrillt** *(geh-grilt)* . . . . grilled _____
□ **paniert** *(pan-neert)* . . . . breaded _____
□ **gefüllt** *(geh-fewlt)* . . . . stuffed _____

Hier ist an example of what **Sie** might select for your evening meal. Using your menu guide on pages 117 and 118, as well as what **Sie** have learned in this Step, fill in the blanks *in English* with what **Sie** believe your **Kellner** will bring you. **Die Antworten sind** below.

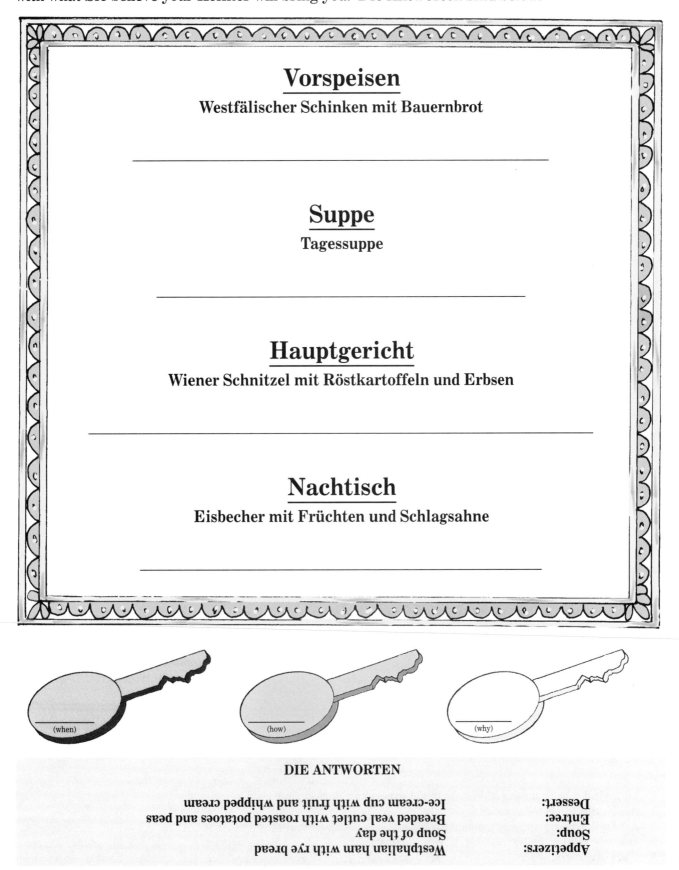

Vorspeisen
Westfälischer Schinken mit Bauernbrot

_____

Suppe
Tagessuppe

_____

Hauptgericht
Wiener Schnitzel mit Röstkartoffeln und Erbsen

_____

Nachtisch
Eisbecher mit Früchten und Schlagsahne

_____

(when)   (how)   (why)

DIE ANTWORTEN

Appetizers:	Westphalian ham with rye bread
Soup:	Soup of the day
Entree:	Breaded veal cutlet with roasted potatoes and peas
Dessert:	Ice-cream cup with fruit and whipped cream

Nun ist a good time for a quick review. Draw lines between **die deutschen Wörter und** their English equivalents.

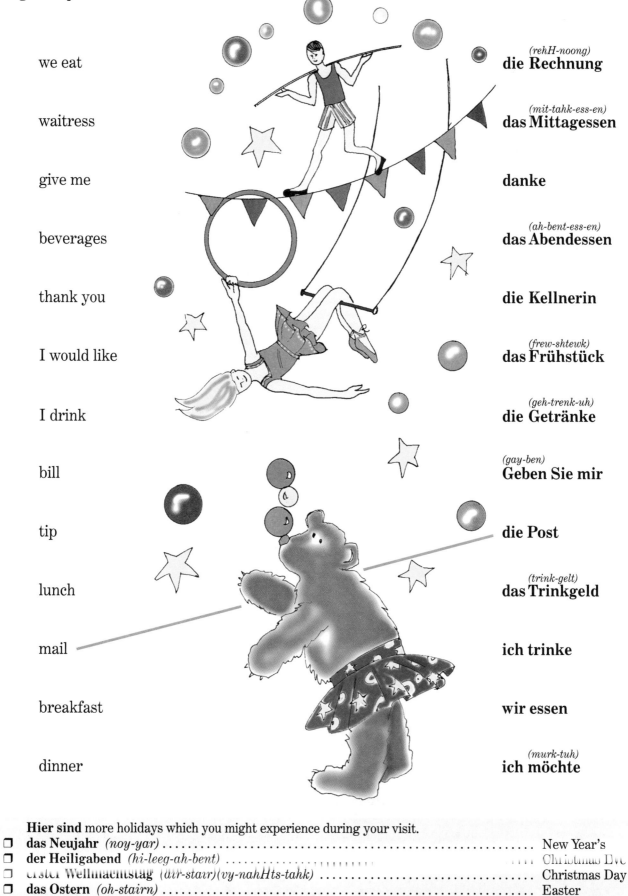

we eat

waitress

give me

beverages

thank you

I would like

I drink

bill

tip

lunch

mail

breakfast

dinner

(rehH-noong)
die Rechnung

(mit-tahk-ess-en)
das Mittagessen

danke

(ah-bent-ess-en)
das Abendessen

die Kellnerin

(frew-shtewk)
das Frühstück

(geh-trenk-uh)
die Getränke

(gay-ben)
Geben Sie mir

die Post

(trink-gelt)
das Trinkgeld

ich trinke

wir essen

(murk-tuh)
ich möchte

Hier sind more holidays which you might experience during your visit.
- ❏ **das Neujahr** *(noy-yar)* . . . . New Year's
- ❏ **der Heiligabend** *(hi-leeg-ah-bent)* . . . . Christmas Eve
- ❏ **erster Weihnachtstag** *(air-stair)(vy-nahHts-tahk)* . . . . Christmas Day
- ❏ **das Ostern** *(oh-stairn)* . . . . Easter

92

Das Telefon
(tay-lay-fohn)
telephone

Was ist different about **das Telefon in** **Deutschland?** *(doych-lahnt)* Well, **Sie** never notice such things until

Sie want to use them. **Telefone** *(tay-lay-foh-nuh)* telephones allow you to call **Freunde,** *(froyn-duh)* friends reserve **Theaterkarten,** *(tay-ah-tair-kar-ten)* theater tickets

Konzertkarten, *(kohn-tsairt-kar-ten)* **Ballettkarten,** *(bah-let-kar-ten)* make emergency calls, check on the hours of a **Museum,** *(moo-zay-oom)* rent

ein Auto *(ow-toh)* **und** all those other **Dinge** which **wir machen** *(mah-Hen)* do on a daily basis. It also gives you a

certain amount of freedom when **Sie können** your own calls **machen.** *(mah-Hen)* make Many travelers use their

Handy *(hen-dee)* cell phone to make these calls.

Telefone *(tay-lay-foh-nuh)* can usually be found everywhere:

in the **Post,** post office on the street, in cafes, at the

Bahnhof *(bahn-hohf)* and in the lobby of your **Hotel.**

The instructions can look complicated,

but remember, **Sie** should be able to

recognize some of these **Wörter** already.

Most **Telefone** use eine **Telefonkarte.** *(tay-lay-fohn-kar-tuh)* telephone card

Sie können *(kur-nen)* buy these **Telefonkarten** at

newsstands as well as at the **Post und am** *(ahm)* at the

Bahnhof. *(bahn-hohf)* train station Ready? Well, before you turn

the page it would be a good idea to go back

und review all your numbers one more time.

To dial from the United States to most other countries **Sie** need that country's international

area code. Your **Telefonbuch** *(tay-lay-fohn-booH)* telephone book at home should have a listing of international area codes.

Hier sind some very useful words built around the word „**Telefon**".
- ❏ **das Telefonbuch** *(tay-lay-fohn-booH)* . . . . telephone book
- ❏ **die Telefonzelle** *(tay-lay-fohn-tsel-luh)* . . . . telephone booth
- ❏ **das Telefongespräch** *(tay-lay-fohn-geh-shprayH)* . . . . telephone conversation
- ❏ **telefonieren** *(tay-lay-foh-neer-en)* . . . . to telephone

When **Sie** leave your contact numbers with friends, family **und** business colleagues, **Sie** should include your destination's country code **und** city code whenever possible. For example:

Country Codes		City Codes	
Germany	49	Berlin	30
		München	89
Austria	43	Wien	1
		Innsbruck	512
Switzerland	41	Zürich	44

From within the country, simply dial "0" before the city code. If you prefer, **Sie kann** go to **die**
can
Post oder call **die Telefonistin** in **Ihrem Hotel** for assistance. Tell **die Telefonistin,**
(tay-lay-foh-nee-stin) *(ear-em)* *(tay-lay-foh-nee-stin)*
operator *your*

(nahH) *(shtoot-gart)* *(tay-lay-foh-neer-en)* *(mewn-shen)* *(tay-lay-foh-neer-en)*
„Ich möchte nach Stuttgart telefonieren." **oder** **„Ich möchte nach München telefonieren."**

Now you try it: _____
(I would like to telephone to . . . .)

(nah-muh)
When answering **das Telefon, Sie** pick up the receiver **und** say your **Name,**

(hah-loh) *(ah-pah-raht)* *(hah-loh)*
Hallo, hier ist_____ **am Apparat.** or simply **Hallo,** _____ .
(Ihr Name) *on the* *phone* (Ihr Name)

(vee-dair-hur-en) *(choos)*
When saying goodbye, **Sie sagen, „Auf Wiederhören" oder „Tschüs"** Your turn —
hear from you again *good-bye*

_____
(Hello, here is . . . . on the phone.)

_____   _____
(good-bye)   (hear from you again)

(frah-gen)
Do not forget that **Sie können fragen** . . .
can

(vee) *(feel)* *(tay-lay-fohn-geh-shprayH)* *(fair-eye-neeg-ten)* *(shtah-ten)*
Wie viel kostet ein Telefongespräch nach den Vereinigten Staaten? _____
U.S.A.

(kah-nah-dah)
Wie viel kostet ein Telefongespräch nach Kanada? _____

Hier sind some emergency telephone numbers for Germany.
- ❏ **die Polizei** *(poh-lih-tsy)* . . . . police 110 _____
- ❏ **die Feuerwehr** *(foy-air-vair)* . . . . fire department 112 _____
- ❏ **der Rettungsdienst** *(ret-toongs-deenst)* . . . . rescue service 112 _____
- ❏ **die Auskunft** *(ows-koonft)* . . . . information 11833 _____

Hier sind some sample sentences **für das Telefon.** *(fewr)* Write them in the blanks **unten.**

Ich möchte nach Miami anrufen. *(murk-tuh) (nahH) (my-ah-mee) (ahn-roo-fen)*
to call
_____

Ich möchte Lufthansa in Frankfurt anrufen. *(looft-hahn-zah)* *(ahn-roo-fen)*
_____

Ich möchte einen Arzt anrufen. *(eye-nen) (arts-t)*
doctor
_____

Meine Nummer ist 67-59-48. *(my-nuh) (noo-mair)*
my
_____

Was ist Ihre Telefonnummer? *(vahs) (ear-uh) (tay-lay-fohn-noo-mair)*
what   your
_____

Was ist die Hoteltelefonnummer? *(vahs)* *(hoh-tel-tay-lay-fohn-noo-mair)*
_____

Christina: **Hallo, hier ist Christina Faber. Ich möchte mit Frau Bresler sprechen.** *(fah-bair)* *(bres-lair)*

_____

Sekretärin: **Einen Augenblick. Es tut mir Leid. Es ist besetzt.** *(ow-gen-blick)* *(toot) (light)* *(beh-zets-t)*
one   moment   I'm sorry   busy, occupied

_____

Christina: **Wiederholen Sie das bitte. Sprechen Sie bitte langsamer.** *(vee-dair-hoh-len)* *(lahng-zah-mair)*
repeat   speak   more slowly

_____

Sekretärin: **Es tut mir Leid. Es ist besetzt.** *(toot) (light)* *(beh-zets-t)*

_____

Christina: **Ah. Danke. Auf Wiederhören.** *(owf) (vee-dair-hur-en)*

_____

Sie sind nun ready to use any **Telefon in Deutschland.** Just take it **langsam und** speak clearly. *(lahng-zahm)*
slowly

Hier sind countries **Sie** may wish to call.

❏ **das Australien** *(ow-strah-lee-en)* .... Australia   _____
❏ **das Österreich** *(ur-stair-ry-sh)* .... Austria   _____
❏ **das Belgien** *(bel-gee-en)* .... Belgium   _____
❏ **das Kanada** *(kah-nah-dah)* .... Canada   _____

(oo-bahn) Die U-Bahn
subway

An excellent means of transportation **ist die** *(oo-bahn)* **U-Bahn. Die** *(groh-sen)* **großen** *(shtay-tuh)* **Städte haben eine**
large   cities

U-Bahn. Die *(kly-nair-en)* **kleineren** *(shtay-tuh)* **Städte haben eine** *(shtrah-sen-bahn)* **Straßenbahn.** Both **die U-Bahn und die**
smaller   streetcar

Straßenbahn sind *(ein-fahH)* **einfach und** quick ways to travel. Plus there is always **der Bus.** *(boos)*

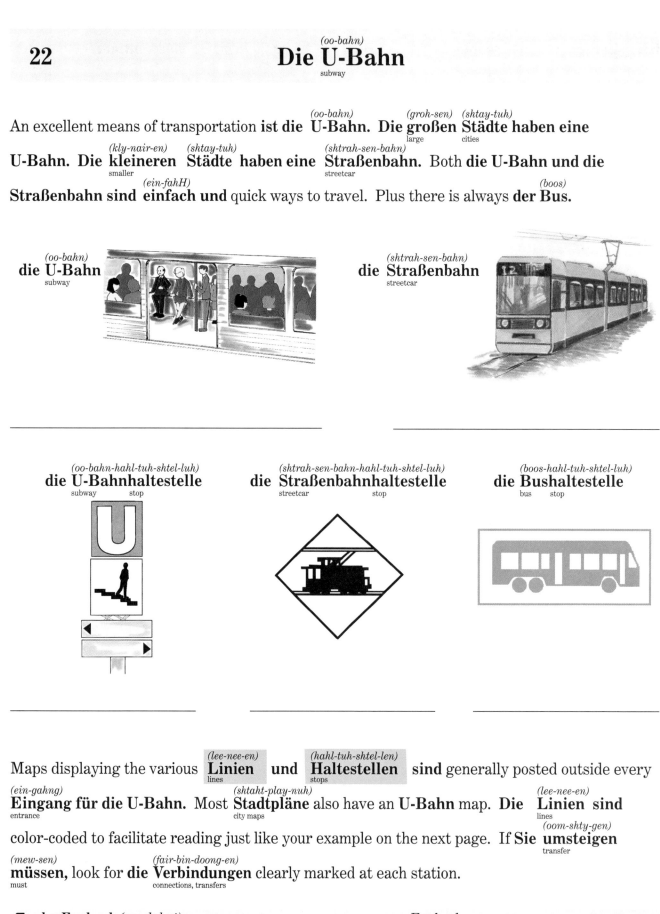

(oo-bahn)
die U-Bahn
subway

(shtrah-sen-bahn)
die Straßenbahn
streetcar

(oo-bahn-hahl-tuh-shtel-luh)
die U-Bahnhaltestelle
subway   stop

(shtrah-sen-bahn-hahl-tuh-shtel-luh)
die Straßenbahnhaltestelle
streetcar   stop

(boos-hahl-tuh-shtel-luh)
die Bushaltestelle
bus   stop

Maps displaying the various *(lee-nee-en)* **Linien und** *(hahl-tuh-shtel-len)* **Haltestellen sind** generally posted outside every
lines   stops

(ein-gahng) **Eingang für die U-Bahn.** Most *(shtaht-play-nuh)* **Stadtpläne** also have an **U-Bahn** map. **Die** *(lee-nee-en)* **Linien sind**
entrance   city maps   lines

color-coded to facilitate reading just like your example on the next page. If **Sie** *(oom-shty-gen)* **umsteigen**
transfer

(mew-sen) **müssen,** look for **die** *(fair-bin-doong-en)* **Verbindungen** clearly marked at each station.
must   connections, transfers

- ❐ **das England** *(eng-lahnt)* . . . . England   _____
- ❐ **das Spanien** *(shpah-nee-en)* . . . . Spain   _____
- ❐ **das Irland** *(ear-lahnt)* . . . . Ireland   _____
- ❐ **das Israel** *(eez-rah-el)* . . . . Israel   _____
- ❐ **das Italien** *(ee-tah-lee-en)* . . . . Italy

Other than having foreign words, **die deutsche U-Bahn** functions just like **in London oder in New York.** Locate your destination, select the correct line on your practice **U-Bahn und** hop on board.

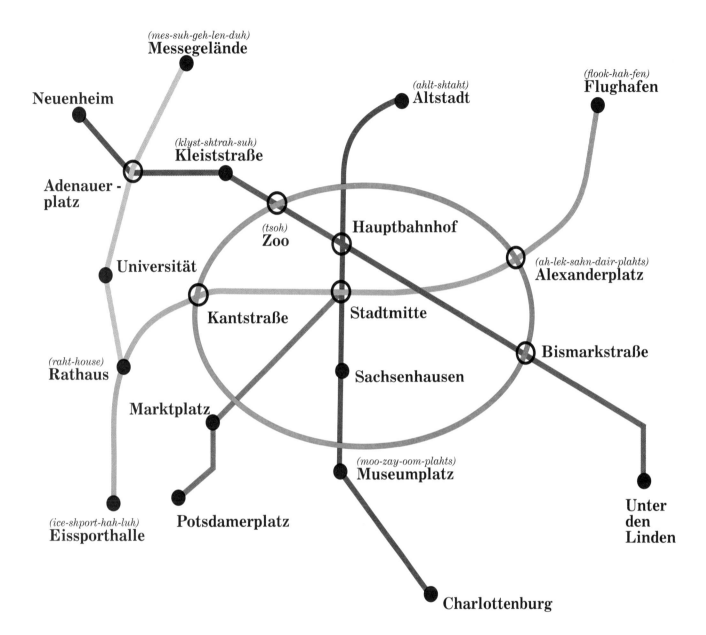

Say these questions aloud many times and don't forget you need **eine Karte für die U-Bahn.**

(oo-bahn-hahl-tuh-shtel-luh)
Wo ist die U-Bahnhaltestelle?

(shtrah-sen-bahn-hahl-tuh-shtel-luh)
Wo ist die Straßenbahnhaltestelle?

(boos-hahl-tuh-shtel-luh)
Wo ist die Bushaltestelle?

❐ **das Frankreich** *(frahnk-ry-sh)* . . . . France . . . .
❐ **das Holland** *(hohl-lahnt)* . . . . Holland . . . .
❐ **das Südafrika** *(zewt-ah-frih-kah)* . . . . South Africa . . . .
❐ **die Schweiz** *(shvites)* . . . . Switzerland . . . .
❐ **die Vereinigten Staaten** *(fair-eye-neeg-ten)(shtah-ten)* United States . . . .

Practice the following basic **Fragen** out loud **und** *(dahn)* **dann** write them in the blanks below.

then

1. *(vee)* *(fairt)* *(tsoor)* *(shtaht-mit-tuh)*
   Wie oft fährt die U-Bahn zur Stadtmitte? _____

   how often travels to the

   (tsoor)
   Wie oft fährt die Straßenbahn zur Stadtmitte? _____

   (boos) *(tsoom)* *(flook-hah-fen)*
   Wie oft fährt der Bus zum Flughafen? _____

2. *(vahn)* *(fairt)* *(ahp)*
   Wann fährt die U-Bahn ab? _____

   when departs

   (vahn)
   Wann fährt die Straßenbahn ab? _____

   (boos)
   Wann fährt der Bus ab? _____

3. *(vee)* *(feel)* *(koh-stet)* *(oo-bahn-kar-tuh)*
   Wie viel kostet eine U-Bahnkarte? _____

   Wie viel kostet eine Straßenbahnkarte? _____

   Wie viel kostet eine Buskarte? _____

4. *(voh)* *(oo-bahn-hahl-tuh-shtel-luh)*
   Wo ist die U-Bahnhaltestelle? _____

   Wo ist die Straßenbahnhaltestelle? _____

   Wo ist die Bushaltestelle? _____

Let's change directions **und** learn **drei** new verbs. **Sie** know the basic "plug-in" formula, so

write out your own sentences using these new verbs.

(vah-shen)
waschen _____

to wash

(fair-lear-en)
verlieren _____

to lose

(dow-airt)
es dauert _____

it lasts, it takes

Hier sind a few more holidays to keep in mind.
- ☐ **der Tag der Arbeit** *(tahk)(dair)(ar-bite)* .... Labor Day (May 1)
- ☐ **der Silvester** *(sil-ves-tair)* .... New Year's Eve
- ☐ **zweiter Weihnachtstag** *(tsvy-tair)(vy-nahkhts-tahk)* .... Dec. 26
- ☐ **das Allerheiligen** *(ahl-lair-hi-lee-gen)* .... All Saints Day (Nov. 1)

98

23

Verkaufen und Kaufen
(fair-kow-fen) selling   *(kow-fen)* buying

Shopping abroad is exciting. The simple everyday task of buying **einen Liter** *(lee-tair)* liter **Milch** *(milsh)* milk **oder einen Apfel** *(ahp-fel)* apple becomes a challenge that **Sie** should **nun** be able to meet quickly **und** easily. Of course, **Sie** will purchase **Andenken,** *(ahn-denk-en)* souvenirs **Briefmarken und Postkarten,** *(breef-mar-ken)* but do not forget those many other items ranging from shoelaces to aspirin that **Sie** might need unexpectedly. Locate your store, draw a line to it **und,** as always, write your new words in the blanks provided.

das Kaufhaus *(kowf-house)* department store _____

das Kino *(kee-noh)* cinema _____

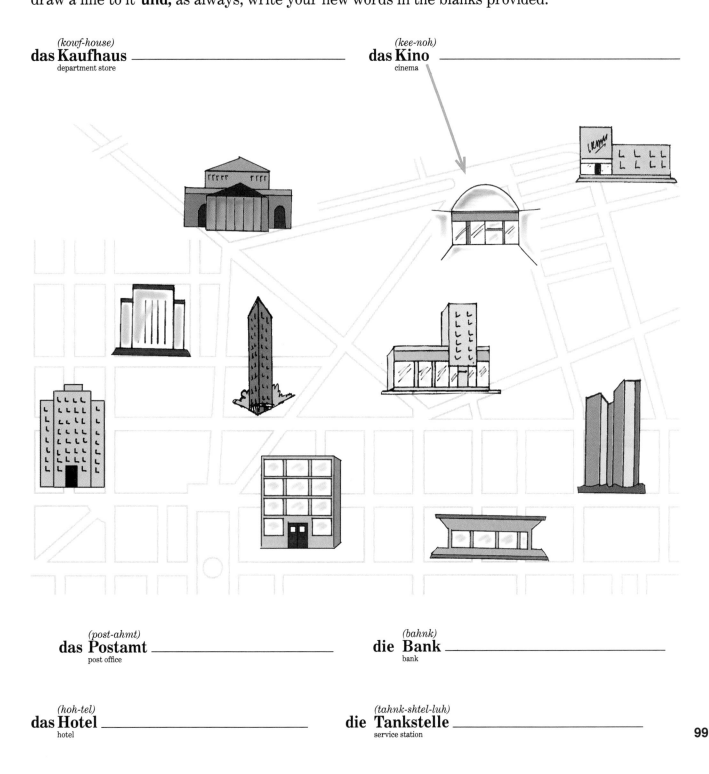

das Postamt *(post-ahmt)* post office _____

die Bank *(bahnk)* bank _____

das Hotel *(hoh-tel)* hotel _____

die Tankstelle *(tahnk-shtel-luh)* service station _____

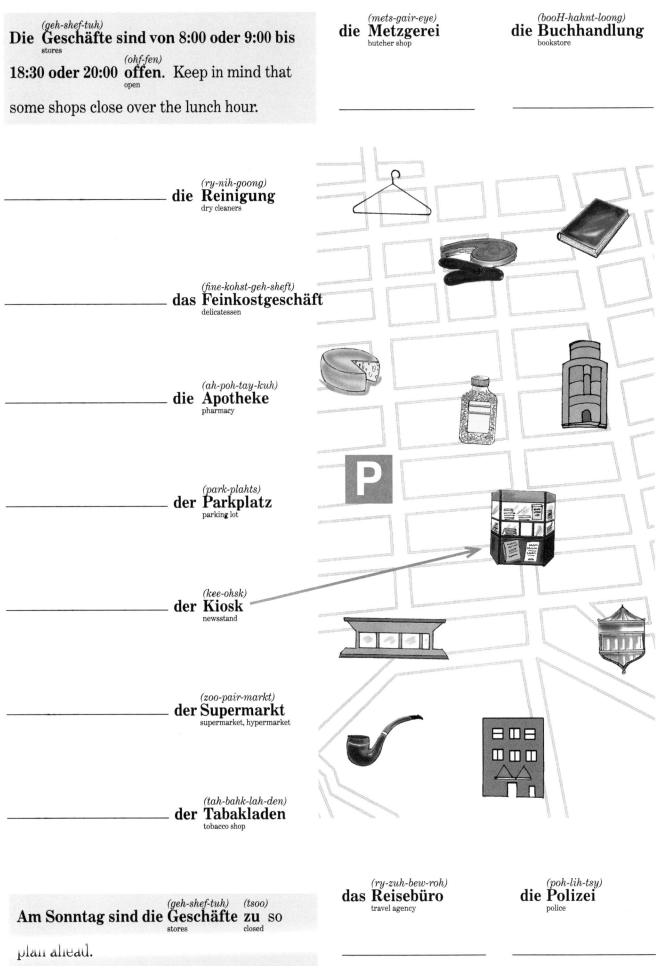

Die **Geschäte** *(geh-shef-tuh)* sind von 8:00 oder 9:00 bis
stores

18:30 oder 20:00 **offen** *(ohf-fen)*. Keep in mind that
open

some shops close over the lunch hour.

(mets-gair-eye)
die **Metzgerei**
butcher shop

(booH-hahnt-loong)
die **Buchhandlung**
bookstore

_____ die **Reinigung** *(ry-nih-goong)*
dry cleaners

_____ das **Feinkostgeschäft** *(fine-kohst-geh-sheft)*
delicatessen

_____ die **Apotheke** *(ah-poh-tay-kuh)*
pharmacy

_____ der **Parkplatz** *(park-plahts)*
parking lot

_____ der **Kiosk** *(kee-ohsk)*
newsstand

_____ der **Supermarkt** *(zoo-pair-markt)*
supermarket, hypermarket

_____ der **Tabakladen** *(tah-bahk-lah-den)*
tobacco shop

(ry-zuh-bew-roh)
das **Reisebüro**
travel agency

(poh-lih-tsy)
die **Polizei**
police

Am Sonntag sind die Geschäte *(geh-shef-tuh)* **zu** *(tsoo)* so
stores closed

plan ahead.

100

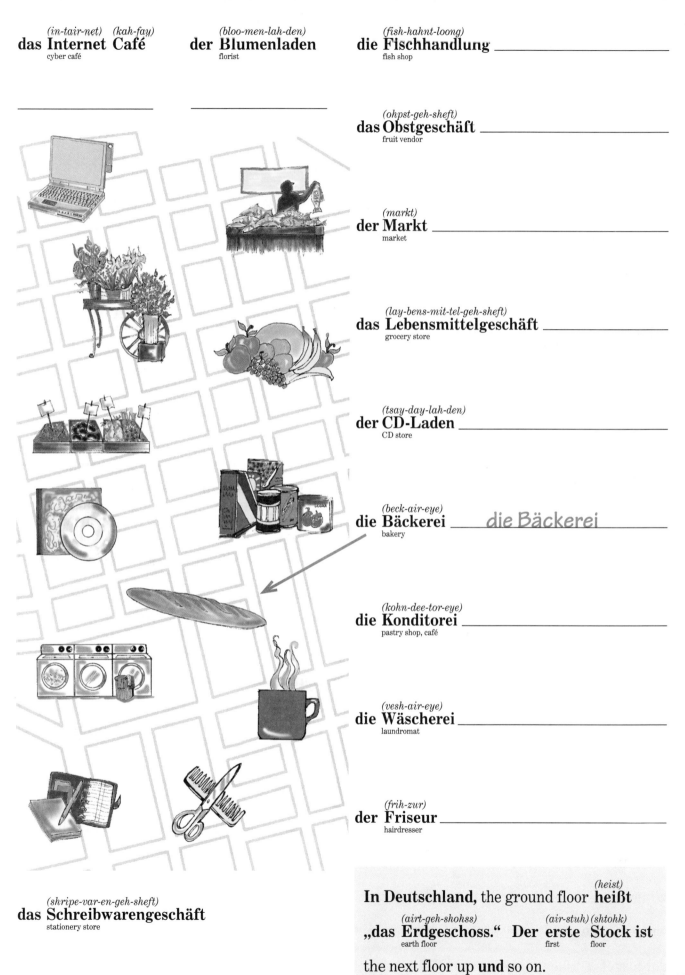

(in-tair-net) (kah-fay)
das Internet Café
cyber café

(bloo-men-lah-den)
der Blumenladen
florist

(fish-hahnt-loong)
die Fischhandlung _____
fish shop

_____

(ohpst-geh-sheft)
das Obstgeschäft _____
fruit vendor

(markt)
der Markt _____
market

(lay-bens-mit-tel-geh-sheft)
das Lebensmittelgeschäft _____
grocery store

(tsay-day-lah-den)
der CD-Laden _____
CD store

(beck-air-eye)
die Bäckerei _____die Bäckerei_____
bakery

(kohn-dee-tor-eye)
die Konditorei _____
pastry shop, café

(vesh-air-eye)
die Wäscherei _____
laundromat

(frih-zur)
der Friseur _____
hairdresser

(shripe-var-en-geh-sheft)
das Schreibwarengeschäft
stationery store

_____

In Deutschland, the ground floor **heißt**
(heist)
(airt-geh-shohss) **(air-stuh) (shtohk)**
„das Erdgeschoss.“ Der erste Stock ist
earth floor   first   floor

the next floor up **und** so on.

24

Das Kaufhaus
(kowf-house)
department store

At this point, **Sie** should just about be ready for **Ihre Reise.** *(ear-uh) (ry-zuh)* **Sie** have gone shopping for those

last-minute odds 'n ends. Most likely, the store directory at your local **Kaufhaus** *(kowf-house)* department store did not look

like the one **unten. Sie wissen** *(viss-en)* know that „**Kind**" *(kint)* is German for "<u>child</u>" so if **Sie brauchen** *(brow-Hen)*

something for a child, **Sie** would probably look on **Stock zwei oder drei,** *(shtohk)* floor wouldn't you?

4. STOCK	Restaurant Fundbüro Kundendienst Reisebüro	Foto Hobby Bücher Multimedia	Toiletten Autozubehör Tierbedarf Sport
3. STOCK	Kindermöbel Kinderwagen Spielwaren Elektrogeräte	Lampen Betten Küchenmöbel Haushalt	Teppiche Bettwäsche Gardinen Bestecke
2. STOCK	Kinderbekleidung Glas Keramik Musikinstrumente	Herrenbekleidung Herrenschuhe Herrenhüte Koffer	Bilder Geschenkartikel Schreibwaren Bürobedarf
1. STOCK	Damenbekleidung Damenschuhe Damenwäsche Damenhüte	Strümpfe Badeartikel Gürtel Nähartikel	Schirme Schlüsselbar Café
E	Lebensmittel Zeitschriften Süßwaren Uhren	Delikatessen Zeitungen Schmuck Parfümerie	Weine Tabakwaren Blumen Lederwaren

Let's start a checklist **für Ihre Reise.** *(ear-uh)* your Besides **Kleider, was brauchen Sie?** *(kly-dair)* clothing *(vahs) (brow-Hen)* As you learn

these **Wörter,** assemble these items **in einer Ecke** *(eck-uh)* corner of your **Haus.** Check **und** make sure that

they **sind sauber und** *(zow-bair)* clean ready **für Ihre Reise.** *(ear-uh)* Be sure to do the same **mit** with the rest of the

Dinge things that **Sie packen.** *(pah-ken)* On the next pages, match each item to its picture, draw a line to it and

write out the word many times. As **Sie** organize these things, check them off on this list. Do

not forget to take the next group of sticky labels and label these **Dinge heute.** today

der Pass *(pahss)*
passport

die Karte *(kar-tuh)*
ticket

der Koffer *(koh-fair)*
suitcase

der Koffer, der Koffer, der Koffer ☑

die Handtasche *(hahnt-tah-shuh)*
handbag

die Brieftasche *(breef-tah-shuh)*
wallet

das Geld *(gelt)*
money

die Kreditkarten *(kray-deet-kar-ten)*
credit cards

die Reiseschecks *(ry-zuh-shecks)*
traveler's checks

die Kamera *(kah-mair-ah)*
camera

die Batterien *(bah-tair-ee-en)*
batteries

die Badehose *(bah-duh-hoh-zuh)*
swimming trunks

der Badeanzug *(bah-duh-ahn-tsook)*
swimsuit

die Sandalen *(zahn-dah-len)*
sandals

die Sonnenbrille *(zoh-nen-bril-luh)*
sunglasses

die Zahnbürste *(tsahn-bewr-stuh)*
toothbrush

die Zahnpasta *(tsahn-pah-stah)*
toothpaste

die Seife *(zy-fuh)*
soap

das Rasiermesser *(rah-zeer-mes-air)*
razor

das Deo *(day-oh)*
deodorant

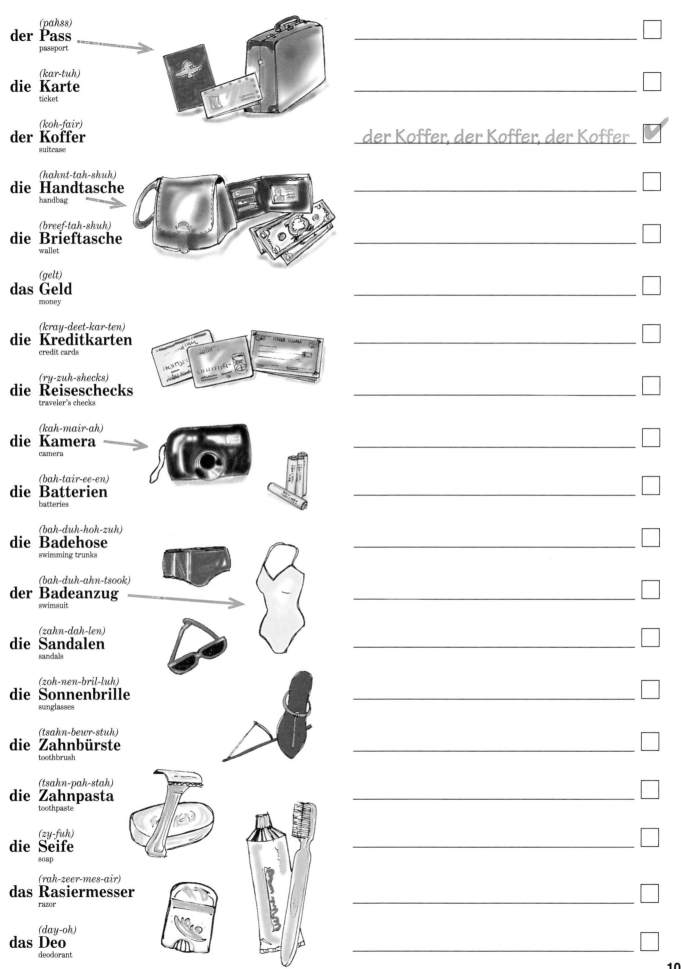

der Kamm *(kahm)*
comb

der Kamm, der Kamm, der Kamm ✓

der Regenmantel *(ray-gen-mahn-tel)*
raincoat

der Regenschirm *(ray-gen-shirm)*
umbrella

der Mantel *(mahn-tel)*
coat

die Handschuhe *(hahnt-shoo-uh)*
gloves

die Mütze *(mewt-suh)*
cap

der Hut *(hoot)*
hat

die Stiefel *(shtee-fel)*
boots

die Schuhe *(schoo-uh)*
shoes

die Tennisschuhe *(ten-is-shoo-uh)*
tennis shoes

der Anzug *(ahn-tsook)*
suit

die Krawatte *(krah-vah-tuh)*
tie

das Hemd *(hemt)*
shirt

das Taschentuch *(tah-shen-tooH)*
handkerchief

die Jacke *(yah-kuh)*
jacket, blazer

die Hose *(hoh-zuh)*
trousers

die Jeans *(jeans)*
jeans

die Shorts *(shorts)*
shorts

das T-Shirt *(tee-shirt)*
t-shirt

die Unterhose *(oon-tair-hoh-zuh)*
underpants

das Unterhemd *(oon-tair-hemt)*
undershirt

das Kleid *(klite)*
dress

die Bluse *(bloo-zuh)*
blouse

der Rock *(rohk)*
skirt

der Rock, der Rock, der Rock ✓

der Pulli *(poo-lee)*
sweater

der Unterrock *(oon-tair-rohk)*
slip

der BH *(bay-hah)*
bra

die Unterhose *(oon-tair-hoh-zuh)*
underpants

die Socken *(zoh-ken)*
socks

die Strumpfhose *(shtroomf-hoh-zuh)*
pantyhose

der Schlafanzug *(shlahf-ahn-tsook)*
pajamas

das Nachthemd *(nahHt-hemt)*
nightshirt

der Bademantel *(bah-duh-mahn-tel)*
bathrobe

die Hausschuhe *(house-shoo-uh)*
slippers

From now on, **Sie haben „Seife" und nicht** "soap." *(zy-fuh)* Having assembled these **Dinge, Sie sind** ready **reisen.** Let's add these important shopping phrases to your basic repertoire.
to travel

Welche Größe? *(vel-chuh) (gruh-suh)* _____
which   size

Es passt. *(pahst)* _____
it   fits

Es passt nicht. *(pahst)* _____
it   does not fit

Treat yourself to a final review. **Sie** know **die Namen für die deutschen Geschäfte,** so let's practice shopping. Just remember your key question **Wörter** that you learned in Step 2. Whether **Sie** need to buy **einen Hut** (hoot) **oder ein Buch** the necessary **Wörter sind** the same.

1. First step — **Wo?** (voh)

Wo ist die Bank? (bahnk)   **Wo ist das Kino?** (kee-noh)   **Wo ist der Kiosk?** (kee-ohsk)

_____

(Where is the department store?)

_____

(Where is the grocery store?)

_____

(Where is the market?)

2. Second step — tell them what **Sie** are looking for, need **oder möchten!**

Ich brauche . . . (brow-Huh)
need
     Ich möchte . . . (murk-tuh)
would like
     Haben Sie . . . ? (hah-ben)
do you have

_____

(Do you have postcards?)

_____

(I would like four stamps.)

_____

(I need toothpaste.)

_____

(I would like to buy batteries.)

_____

(Do you have coffee?)

Go through the glossary at the end of this **Buch und** select **zwanzig Wörter.** Drill the above

(dee-zen)
patterns **mit diesen zwanzig Wörtern.** Don't cheat. Drill them **heute. Nun,** take **zwanzig**

these

(ear-em) *(vur-tair-booH)*
more **Wörter von Ihrem Wörterbuch und** do the same.

your   dictionary

(vee) (feel)
3. Third step — find out **wie viel es kostet.**

(vee) (feel) *(dahs)*	*(koh-stet)*	*(bilt)*
Wie viel kostet das?	**Wie viel kostet die Postkarte?**	**Wie viel kostet das Bild?**

_____

(How much does the newspaper cost?)

_____

(How much does the soap cost?)

_____

(How much does a cup of tea cost?)

4.   Fourth step — success! I found it!

(zah-gen)
Once **Sie finden** what **Sie** would like, **Sie sagen,**

say

Ich möchte das bitte. _Ich möchte das bitte. Ich möchte das bitte._ ___

or

(nay-muh)
Ich nehme das bitte. _____

take

Oder if **Sie** would not like it, **Sie sagen,**

(neeHt)
Ich möchte das nicht. _____

or

(nay-muh)
Ich nehme das nicht. _____

do not take

Congratulations! You have finished. By now you should have stuck your labels, flashed your

cards, cut out your menu guide and packed your suitcases. You should be very pleased with your

accomplishment. You have learned what it sometimes takes others years to achieve and you

(goo-tuh) (ry-zuh)
hopefully had fun doing it. **Gute Reise!**

Glossary

This glossary contains words used in this book only. It is not meant to be a dictionary. Consider purchasing a dictionary which best suits your needs—small for traveling, large for reference, or specialized for specific vocabulary needs.

A

Abend, der *(ah-bent)*.....................evening
Abendessen, das *(ah-bent-ess-en)*...........dinner
abends *(ah-bents)*......... evenings, in the evening
abfahren *(ahp-far-en)*.............to depart, leave
Abfahrt, die *(ahp-fahrt)*..............departure
Abteil, das *(ahp-tile)*.............compartment
acht *(ahHt)*.........................eight
achtzehn *(ahHt-tsayn)*...............eighteen
achtzig *(ahHt-tsig)*..................eighty
Adresse, die *(ah-dres-suh)*..............address
Akademie, die *(ah-kah-deh-mee)*.........academy
Akt, der *(ahkt)*.................act (of a play)
Akzent, der *(ahk-tsent)*..................accent
Alkohol, die *(ahl-koh-hohl)*............ alcohol
alle *(ahl-luh)*................all, everyone
alles *(ahl-les)*.................everything
Alpen, die *(ahl-pen)*..................the Alps
Alphabet, das *(ahl-fah-bate)*.............alphabet
alt *(ahlt)*...........................old
am *(= an dem)*.................at the, on the
Amerika, das *(ah-mair-ih-kah)*..........America
Amerikaner, der *(ah-mair-ih-kahn-air)*.. American
an *(ahn)*............ on, upon (vertical surfaces), at
Andenken, das *(ahn-denk-en)*...........souvenir
ankommen *(ahn-koh-men)*..............to arrive
Ankunft, die *(ahn-koonft)*................arrival
Anruf, der *(ahn-roof)*.........call, telephone call
anrufen *(ahn-roo-fen)*................to call
Anschrift, die *(ahn-shrift)*..............address
Antwort, die *(ahnt-vort)*................answer
Anzug, der *(ahn-tsook)*...................suit
Apfel, der *(ahp-fel)*......................apple
Apotheke, die *(ah-poh-tay-kuh)*.........pharmacy
Apparat, der *(ah-pah-raht)*.....telephone, receiver
Appetit, der *(ah-peh-teet)*...............appetite
April, der *(ah-pril)*.......................April
arm *(arm)*............................poor
Arzt, der *(arts-t)*.......................physician
auch *(owH)*...........................also
auf *(owf)*......on top of (horizontal surfaces), open
auf Deutsch *(owf)(doych)*.............in German
Auf Wiederhören! *(owf)(vee-dair-hur-en)*.........
.....................Hear from you again!
Auf Wiedersehen! *(owf)(vee-dair-zay-en)*.........
....................See you again!, good-bye
Aufschnitt, der *(owf-shnit)*..............cold cuts
aufschreiben *(owf-shry-ben)*..........to write out
Augenblick, der *(ow-gen-blick)*...........moment
August, der *(ow-goost)*..................August
aus *(ows)*...........................out of, from
Ausfahrt, die *(ows-fahrt)*.......exit (for vehicles)
Ausgang, der *(ows-gahng)*.........exit (for people)
Auskunft, die *(ows-koonft)*...........information
Ausland, das *(ows-lahnt)*...abroad, foreign country

Australien, das *(ow-shtrah-lee-en)*.......Australia
Auto, das *(ow-toh) (die Autos)*.................car
Autobahn, die *(ow-toh-bahn)*............freeway
Autor, der *(ow-tor)*......................author

B

BH, der *(bay-hah)*.........................bra
Bäckerei, die *(beck-air-eye)*...............bakery
Bad, das *(baht)*.................bath, bathroom
Badeanzug, der *(bah-duh-ahn-tsook)*.. bathing suit
Badehose, die *(bah-duh-hoh-zuh)*..swimming trunks
Bademantel, der *(bah-duh-mahn-tel)*.....bathrobe
baden *(bah-den)*.......................to bathe
Badezimmer, das *(bah-duh-tsih-mair)*...bathroom
Bahnhof, der *(bahn-hohf)*.............train station
Bahnsteig, der *(bahn-shtaig)*.....railway platform
Ball, der *(bahl)*.........................ball
Ballett, das *(bah-let)*....................ballet
Ballettkarte, die *(bah-let-kar-tuh)*.....ballet ticket
Banane, die *(bah-nah-nuh)*..............banana
Bank, die *(bahnk)*.......................bank
Batterie, die *(bah-tair-ee)*................battery
Bedienung, die *(beh-dee-noong)*....service charge
Beefsteak, das *(beef-steak)*..............beefsteak
Belgien, das *(bel-gee-en)*.............. Belgium
besetzt *(beh-zets-t)*.....................occupied
besser *(bes-air)*........................better
bestellen *(beh-shtel-len)*.................to order
Bett, das *(bet)*..........................bed
Bettdecke, die *(bet-deck-uh)*....blanket, bedspread
bezahlen *(beh-tsah-len)*.................to pay
Bier, das *(beer)*.........................beer
Bierstein, der *(beer-stein)*............beer mug
Bild, das *(bilt)*.........................picture
billig *(bil-lig)*...........................cheap
bin *(bin)*............................(I) am
bitte *(bit-tuh)*...........please, you're welcome
bitte schön *(bit-tuh)(shurn)*..you're very welcome
blau *(blau)*............................blue
bleiben *(bly-ben)*.............to remain, stay
Bleistift, der *(bly-shtift)*.................pencil
Blume, die *(bloo-muh)*...................flower
Blumenladen, der *(bloo-men-lah-den)*...flower shop
Bluse, die *(bloo-zuh)*...................blouse
Boot, das *(boht)*........................boat
brauchen *(brow-Hen)*.................to need
braun *(brown)*........................brown
Brief, der *(breef)*.......................letter
Briefkasten, der *(breef-kah-sten)*.........mailbox
Briefmarke, die *(breef-mar-kuh)*..........stamp
Brieftasche, die *(breef-tah-shuh)*..........wallet
Brille, die *(bril-luh)*..................eyeglasses
bringen *(bring-en)*....................to bring
Brot, das *(broht)*.......................bread
Brötchen, das *(brurt-chen)*................roll
Bruder, der *(broo-dair)*.................brother

Buch, das (booH) . . . . book
Buchhandlung, die (booH-hahnt-loong) . . bookstore
bunt (boont) . . . . multi-colored
Büro, das (bew-roh) . . . . office, study
Bus, der (boos) . . . . bus
Bushaltestelle, die (boos-hahl-tuh-shtel-luh) . . . . . .
. . . . bus stop
Butter, die (boo-tair) . . . . butter

C

Café, das (kah-fay) . . . . café
CD-Laden, der (tsay-day-lah-den) . . . . CD store
Celsius, das (sel-see-oos) . . . . centigrade
Champagner, der (shahm-pahn-yair) . . champagne
Chemie, die (shay-mee) . . . . chemistry
Chile, das (she-lay) . . . . Chile
China, das (she-nah) . . . . China
chinesisch (she-nay-zish) . . . . Chinese
Chor, der (kor) . . . . choir
christlich (krist-leeH) . . . . Christian
Computer, der (kohm-pyoo-tair) . . . . computer

D

Dame, die (dah-muh) . . . . lady
Dänemark, das (day-nuh-mark) . . . . Denmark
Dänisch, das (day-nish) . . . . Danish (language)
danke (dahn-kuh) . . . . thank you
danke schön (dahn-kuh)(shurn) . . . .
. . . . thank you very much
dann (dahn) . . . . then
das (dahs) . . . . the, that
dauert (dow-airt) . . . . (it) lasts, takes
dem (dehm) . . . . the
den (dehn) . . . . the
Deo, das (day-oh) . . . . deodorant
der (dair) . . . . the, of the
des (des) . . . . the, of the
Deutsch, das (doych) . . . . German (language)
deutsch (doych) . . . . German
deutsche (doy-chuh) . . . . German
Deutschen, die (doy-chen) . . . . German people
Deutschland, das (doych-lahnt) . . . . Germany
Dezember, der (day-tsem-bair) . . . . December
die (dee) . . . . the
Dienstag, der (deens-tahk) . . . . Tuesday
diesen (dee-zen) . . . . this, these
Ding, das (ding) . . . . thing
Doktor, der (dohk-tor) . . . . doctor (title)
Donnerstag, der (doh-nairs-tahk) . . . . . . Thursday
dort (dort) . . . . there
drei (dry) . . . . three
dreißig (dry-sig) . . . . thirty
dreizehn (dry-tsayn) . . . . thirteen
Drogerie, die (droh-geh-ree) . . . . drugstore
drücken (drew-ken) . . . . to push (doors)
du (doo) . . . . you (informal, singular)
Durst, der (doorst) . . . . thirst
Dusche, die (doosh-uh) . . . . shower

E

€ . . . . abbreviation for "Euro"
Ecke, die (eck-uh) . . . . corner
Ei, das (eye) . . . . egg
Eierspeisen, die (eye-air-shpy-zen) . . . . . egg dishes

ein (ein) . . . . a
ein bisschen (ein)(bis-Hen) . . . . a little
ein Paar (ein) (par) . . . . a pair, a couple
eine (eye-nuh) . . . . a
einem (eye-nem) . . . . a, to a
einen (eye-nen) . . . . a
einer (eye-nair) . . . . a, of a
eines (eye-nes) . . . . a, of a
einfach (ein-fahH) . . . . one-way, simple
Einfahrt, die (ein-fahrt) . . . . . entrance (for vehicles)
Eingang, der (ein-gahng) . . . . . entrance (for people)
eins (eins) . . . . one
Eis, das (ice) . . . . ice cream
Elefant, der (ay-lay-fahnt) . . . . elephant
elf (elf) . . . . eleven
Eltern, die (el-tairn) . . . . parents
Email, die (ee-mail) . . . . email
England, das (eng-lahnt) . . . . England
Engländer, der (eng-len-dair) . . . . . . English (male)
Englisch, das (eng-lish) . . . . English (language)
Entschuldigung (ent-shool-dee-goong) . . excuse me
er (air) . . . . he
Erdgeschoss, das (airt-geh-shohss) . . . . ground floor
erste (air-stuh) . . . . first
es (es) . . . . it
es gibt (es)(gipt) . . . . there is, there are
es tut mir Leid (es)(toot)(mir)(light) . . . . I am sorry
essen (ess-en) . . . . to eat
Essen, das (ess-en) . . . . meal
Esszimmer, das (ess-tsih-mair) . . . . dining room
Euro, der (oy-roh) . . . . euro
Europa, das (oy-roh-pah) . . . . Europe
europäisch (oy-roh-pay-ish) . . . . European
evangelisch (ay-vahn-gay-lish) . . . . Protestant

F

fahren (fah-ren) . . . . to go, drive, travel
Fahrenheit, die (fah-ren-hite) . . . . Fahrenheit
Fahrkarte, die (far-kar-tuh) . . . . ticket
Fahrplan, der (far-plahn) . . . . timetable
Fahrrad, das (far-raht) . . . . bicycle
Familie, die (fah-mee-lee-uh) . . . . family
fantastisch (fahn-tahs-tish) . . . . fantastic
Farbe, die (far-buh) . . . . color
Fax, das (fahks) . . . . fax
Februar, der (fay-broo-ar) . . . . February
Feinkostgeschäft, das (fine-kohst-geh-sheft) . . . .
. . . . delicatessen
Fenster, das (fehn-stair) . . . . window
Ferngespräch, das (fairn-geh-shprayH) . . . .
. . . . long-distance telephone call
Fernseher, der (fairn-zay-air) . . . . television set
Feuerwehr, die (foy-air-vair) . . . . . . fire department
Film, der (film) . . . . film
finden (fin-den) . . . . to find
Finger, der (fing-air) . . . . finger
Fisch, der (fish) . . . . fish
Fischgerichte, die (fish-geh-reeH-tuh) . . fish entrees
Fischhandlung, die (fish-hahnt-loong) . . . fish store
Flasche, die (flah-shuh) . . . . bottle
Fleisch, das (fly-sh) . . . . meat
fliegen (flee-gen) . . . . to fly
Flug, der (flook) . . . . flight
Flughafen, der (flook-hah-fen) . . . . airport
Flugkarte, die (flook-kar-tuh) . . . . . . airplane ticket

Flugzeug, das *(flook-tsoyk)* . . . . airplane
Foto, das *(foh-toh)* . . . . photo
Frage, die *(frah-guh)* . . . . question
fragen *(frah-gen)* . . . . to ask
Frankreich, das *(frahnk-ry-sh)* . . . . France
Französisch, das *(frahn-tsur-zish)* . . French (language)
Frau, die *(frow)* . . . . woman, Mrs., Ms.
Fräulein, das *(froy-line)* . . . . young lady, Miss
frei *(fry)* . . . . free of charge, available
Freitag, der *(fry-tahk)* . . . . Friday
Freund, der *(froynt)* . . . . friend
Friseur, der *(frih-zur)* . . . . hairdresser
Frühling, der *(frew-ling)* . . . . spring
Frühstück, das *(frew-shtewk)* . . . . breakfast
Fundbüro, das *(foont-bew-roh)* . . lost-and-found office
fünf *(fewnf)* . . . . five
fünfhundert *(fewnf-hoon-dairt)* . . . . . five hundred
fünfzehn *(fewnf-tsayn)* . . . . fifteen
fünfzig *(fewnf-tsig)* . . . . fifty
für *(fewr)* . . . . for

G

Gabel, die *(gah-bel)* . . . . fork
Garage, die *(gah-rah-zhuh)* . . . . garage
Garten, der *(gar-ten)* . . . . garden, yard
Gasthaus, das *(gahst-house)* . . . . . . restaurant, inn
gebacken *(geh-bah-ken)* . . . . baked
geben *(gay-ben)* . . . . to give
Geben Sie mir . . . *(gay-ben)(zee)(mir)* . . give me . . !
gebraten *(geh-brah-ten)* . . . . roasted, fried
Geflügel, das *(geh-flew-gel)* . . . . poultry
gefüllt *(geh-fewlt)* . . . . stuffed
gegrillt *(geh-grilt)* . . . . grilled
gehen *(gay-en)* . . . . to go
geht *(gate)* . . . . goes
gekocht *(geh-kohHt)* . . . . cooked, boiled
gelb *(gelp)* . . . . yellow
Geld, das *(gelt)* . . . . money
Geldscheine, die *(gelt-shy-nuh)* . . . . . . bank notes
Geldstücke, die *(gelt-shtew-kuh)* . . . . coins
gemischt *(geh-misht)* . . . . mixed
Gemüse, das *(geh-mew-zuh)* . . . . vegetables
geradeaus *(geh-rah-duh-ows)* . . . . straight ahead
Geschäft, das *(geh-sheft)* . . . . store
Geschwindigkeitsbegrenzung, die *(geh-shvin-dig-kites-beh-gren-tsoong)* . . . . speed limit
gesperrt *(geh-shpairt)* . . . . closed, blocked
Gespräch, das *(geh-shprayH)* . . . . . conversation
gestern *(ges-tairn)* . . . . yesterday
gesund *(geh-zoont)* . . . . healthy
Getränke, die *(geh-trenk-uh)* . . . . beverages
Glas, das *(glahs)* . . . . glass
Gleis, das *(glice)* . . . . track
Glück, das *(glewk)* . . . . luck
Goethe *(goor-tuh)* . . . . 18th century writer
Grad, der *(grahd)* . . . . degree
grau *(grau)* . . . . gray
Grill- und Pfannengerichte, die *(gril-oont-fahn-en-geh-reeH-tuh)* . . . . . . grilled and pan-fried entrees
groß *(grohs)* . . . . large, tall
Größe, die *(gruh-suh)* . . . . size
Großmutter, die *(grohs-moo-tair)* . . . grandmother
Großvater, der *(grohs-vah-tair)* . . . . . grandfather
110 **grün** *(grewn)* . . . . green

Gulasch, das *(goo-lahsh)* . . . . goulash
gut, gutes, gute *(goot)(goo-tes)(goo-tuh)* . . . . . good
Gute Nacht *(goo-tuh)(nahHt)* . . . good night
Gute Reise! *(goo-tuh)(ry-zuh)* . . . . Have a good trip!
Guten Abend *(goo-ten)(ah-bent)* . . . . . good evening
Guten Appetit *(goo-ten)(ah-peh-teet)* . . . . enjoy your meal
Guten Morgen *(goo-ten)(mor-gen)* . . . good morning
Guten Tag *(goo-ten)(tahk)* . . . . good day, hello

H

haben *(hah-ben)* . . . . to have
halb *(hahlp)* . . . . half
Halle, die *(hah-luh)* . . . . hall
Haltestelle, die *(hahl-tuh-shtel-luh)* . . . . transportation stop
Hammel, der *(hah-mel)* . . . . sheep
Handschuhe, die *(hahnt-shoo-uh)* . . . . . . gloves
Handtasche, die *(hahnt-tah-shuh)* . . . . . purse
Handy, das *(hen-dee)* . . . . . cell phone, mobile phone
hat *(haht)* . . . . has
Haupteingang, der *(howpt-ein-gahng)* . main entrance
Hauptgerichte, die *(howpt-geh-reeH-tuh)* . . . . main meals, entrees
Haus, das *(house)* . . . . house
Hauschuhe, die *(house-shoo-uh)* . . . . slippers
Heiligabend, der *(hi-leeg-ah-bent)* . . Christmas Eve
heiß *(hice)* . . . . hot
heißen *(hi-sen)* . . . . to be called
Hemd, das *(hemt)* . . . . shirt
Herbst, der *(hairp-st)* . . . . autumn, fall
Herd, der *(hairt)* . . . . stove
Herr, der *(hair)* . . . . gentleman, Mr.
Herr Ober! *(hair)(oh-bair)* . . . . Waiter!
Herrn *(hairn)* . . . . to Mr.
heute *(hoy-tuh)* . . . . today
hier *(here)* . . . . here
Hilfe! *(hil-fuh)* . . . . help!
hin und zurück *(hin)(oont)(tsoo-rewk)* . . there and back
hinter *(hin-tair)* . . . . behind
hoch *(hohH)* . . . . high
Holland, das *(hohl-lahnt)* . the Netherlands, Holland
Hose, die *(hoh-zuh)* . . . . trousers
Hotel, das *(hoh-tel)* . . . . hotel
Hotelzimmer, das *(hoh-tel-tsih-mair)* . . . hotel room
Hund, der *(hoont)* . . . . dog
hundert *(hoon-dairt)* . . . . hundred
Hunger, der *(hoong-air)* . . . . hunger
Hut, der *(hoot)* . . . . hat

I

ich *(eeH)* I
Idee, die *(ee-day)* . . . . idea
Ihnen *(ee-nen)* . . . . to you
ihr *(ear)* . . . . you (informal, plural)
Ihr, Ihre, Ihrem *(eur)(eur-uh)(ear-em)* . . . . your
im *(= in dem)* . . . . in, in the
im Backteig *(im)(bahk-taig)* . . . . . . in batter, dough
in *(in)* . . . . in
Information, die *(in-for-mah-tsee-ohn)* . information
Inland, das *(in-lahnt)* . . . . . . inland, domestic
Institut, das *(in-stee-toot)* . . . . institute
interessant *(in-tair-es-sahnt)* . . . . interesting
Internet Café, das *(in-tair-net)(kah-fay)* . . cyber café

InterregioExpress, der *(in-tair-ray-gee-oh-eks-press)*
.... medium speed train
Irland, das *(ear-lahnt)* .... Ireland
Israel, das *(eez-rah-el)* .... Israel
ist *(ist)* .... is
Italien, das *(ee-tah-lee-en)* .... Italy
Italienisch, das *(ee-tah-lee-ay-nish)* .. Italian (language)

J

ja *(yah)* .... yes
Jacke, die *(yah-kuh)* .... jacket
Jahr, das *(yar)* .... year
Januar, der *(yah-noo-ar)* .... January
Japan, das *(yah-pahn)* .... Japan
Japanisch, das *(yah-pah-nish)* ... Japanese (language)
Jeans, die *(jeans)* .... jeans
jetzt *(yets-t)* .... now
Journal, das *(zhoor-nahl)* ...... journal, magazine
jüdisch *(yew-dish)* .... Jewish
Juli, der *(yoo-lee)* .... July
jung *(yoong)* .... young
Juni, der *(yoo-nee)* .... June

K

Kabine, die *(kah-bee-nuh)* .... booth
Kaffee, der *(kah-fay)* .... coffee
Kaffeehaus, das *(kah-fay-house)* ... coffee house
Kakao, der *(kah-kow)* .... hot chocolate
Kalender, der *(kah-len-dair)* .... calendar
kalt *(kahlt)* .... cold
Kamera, die *(kah-mair-uh)* .... camera
Kamm, der *(kahm)* .... comb
Kanada, das *(kah-nah-dah)* .... Canada
Kanadier, der *(kah-nah-dyair)* .... Canadian (male)
kann *(kahn)* .... he, she, it can
Kännchen, das *(ken-chen)* ... small coffee or tea pot
Karotten, die *(kah-roh-ten)* .... carrots
Karte, die *(kar-tuh)* ...... card, ticket, map
Kartoffeln, die *(kar-toh-feln)* .... potatoes
Käse, der *(kay-zuh)* .... cheese
Kasse, die *(kah-suh)* .... cashier
katholisch *(kah-toh-lish)* .... Catholic
Katze, die *(kah-tsuh)* .... cat
Kaufhaus, das *(kowf-house)* ..... department store
kaufen *(kow-fen)* .... to buy
kein *(kine)* .... no
Keller, der *(kel-air)* ....cellar
Kellner, der *(kel-nair)* .... waiter
Kellnerin, die *(kel-nair-in)* .... waitress
Kilometer, der *(kee-loh-may-tair)* .... kilometer
Kind, das *(kint)* .... child
Kino, das *(kee-noh)* .... movie theater
Kiosk, der *(kee-ohsk)* .... newsstand
Kirche, die *(kir-Huh)* .... church
Kleid, das *(klite)* .... dress,
Kleiderschrank, der *(kly-dair-shrahnk)* ..clothes closet
klein *(kline)* .... small, short
kochen *(koh-Hen)* .... to cook
Koffer, der *(koh-fair)* .... suitcase
kommen *(koh-men)* .... to come
kommt *(kohmt)* .... comes
Konditorei, die *(kohn-dee-tor-eye)* .pastry shop, café
können *(kur-nen)* .... to be able to, can
Konversation, die *(kohn-vair-zah-tsee-ohn)* ....
.... conversation

Konzert, das *(kohn-tsairt)* .... concert
Konzertkarte, die *(kohn-tsairt-kar-tuh)* .. concert ticket
Kopfkissen, das *(kohpf-kiss-en)* .... pillow
kosten *(koh-sten)* .... to cost
kostet *(koh-stet)* .... costs
Kotelett, das *(koh-teh-let)* .... cutlet, chop
krank *(krahnk)* .... sick, ill
Krawatte, die *(krah-vah-tuh)* .... tie
Kreditkarten, die *(kray-deet-kar-ten)* .. credit cards
Kreuzworträtsel, das *(kroits-vort-rate-sel)* ....
.... crossword puzzle
Kroatien, das *(kroh-aht-zee-en)* .... Croatia
Küche, die *(kew-Huh)* .... kitchen
Kuchen, der *(koo-Hen)* .... cake, pastry
Kuckucksuhr, die *(koo-kooks-oor)* .....cuckoo clock
kühl *(kewl)* .... cool
Kühlschrank, der *(kewl-shrahnk)* ..... refrigerator
Kuli, der *(koo-lee)* .... pen
kurz *(koorts)* .... short

L

Lamm, das *(lahm)* .... lamb
Lampe, die *(lahm-puh)* .... lamp
Land, das *(lahnt)* .... land, country
Landebahn, die *(lahn-duh-bahn)* .... runway
landen *(lahn-den)* .... to land
Landkarte, die *(lahnt-kar-tuh)* .... map
Landung, die *(lahn-doong)* .... landing
lang *(lahng)* .... long
langsam *(lahng-zahm)* ....slow
langsamer *(lahng-zah-mair)* ... slower, more slowly
laut *(lout)* .... loud
Lebensmittelgeschäft, das *(lay-bens-mit-tel-geh-sheft)*
.... grocery store
lernen *(lair-nen)* .... to learn
lesen *(lay-zen)* .... to read
Licht, das *(leeHt)* .... light
Liegewagen, der *(lee-guh-vah-gen)* .. car with berths
Likör, der *(lee-kur)* .... liqueur
Limonade, die *(lee-moh-nah-duh)* .... lemonade
Linie, die *(lee-nee-uh)* .... line
links *(links)* .... left
Liter, der *(lee-tair)* .... liter
Löffel, der *(lur-fel)* .... spoon
Lokomotive, die *(loh-koh-moh-tee-vuh)* . locomotive
los *(lohs)* .... wrong
Luftpost, die *(looft-post)* .... airmail
Luxemburg, das *(look-sem-boorg)* .... Luxembourg

M

machen *(mah-Hen)* .... to make, do
Mai, der *(my)* ....May
man *(mahn)* .... one
Mann, der *(mahn)* ....man
Männer, die *(men-air)* ....men
Mantel, der *(mahn-tel)* ....coat
Markt, der *(markt)* .... market
Marmelade, die *(mar-meh-lah-duh)* .. jam, marmalade
März, der *(mairts)* ....March
Mechaniker, der *(may-Hahn-ee-kair)* .... mechanic
mehr *(mair)* .... more
Meile, die *(my-luh)* ....mile

mein, meine *(mine)(my-nuh)* .... my
Menü, das *(men-ew)* ....special meal of the day
Messegelände, das *(mes-suh-geh-len-dah)* ..fairgrounds
Messer, das *(mes-air)* .... knife
Meter, der *(may-tair)* .... meter
Metzgerei, die *(mets-gair-eye)* .... butcher shop
mich *(meeH)*.............................. me
Mietwagen, der *(meet-vah-gen)* .... rental car
Milch, die *(milsh)* ....milk
Mineralwasser, das *(mih-nair-ahl-vah-sair)* ......
.... mineral water
Minute, die *(mee-noo-tuh)*.............. minute
mir *(mir)*........................ to me, me
mit *(mit)*................................with
Mittag, der *(mit-tahk)* .... noon
Mittagessen, das *(mit-tahk-ess-en)* ....lunch
Mitte, die *(mit-tuh)*................... middle
Mitternacht, die *(mit-tair-nahHt)*.......midnight
Mittwoch, der *(mit-vohH)* .... Wednesday
möchte *(murk-tuh)* ...... (I, he, she, it) would like
möchten *(murk-ten)* ......(we, they, you) would like
Moment, der *(moh-ment)*............... moment
Monat, der *(moh-naht)*...............month
Montag, der *(mohn-tahk)*............. Monday
morgen *(mor-gen)* ....tomorrow
Morgen, der *(mor-gen)* .... morning
morgens *(mor-gens)* ..... mornings, in the morning
Moslem *(mohz-lem)* .... Muslim
Motorrad, das *(moh-tor-raht)* ....motorcycle
Mund, der *(moont)* .... mouth
Museum, das *(moo-zay-oom)* .... museum
Musik, die *(moo-zeek)*................. music
muss *(moos)* .... he, she, it must
müssen *(mew-sen)*.............to have to, must
Mutter, die *(moo-tair)*............... mother
Mütze, die *(mewt-suh)* .... cap

N

nach *(nahH)*................... to, after
Nachmittag, der *(nahH-mit-tahk)* ....afternoon
nachmittags *(nahH-mit-tahks)*..................
.... afternoons, in the afternoon
nächst *(nekst)*...........................next
Nacht, die *(nahHt)* ....night
Nachthemd, das *(nahHt-hemt)*.......nightshirt
Nachtisch, der *(nahH-tish)* .... dessert
Name, der *(nah-muh)*.................name
Nation, die *(nah-tsee-ohn)* .... nation
Nationalität, die *(nah-tsee-oh-nahl-ih-tate)*. nationality
natürlich *(nah-tewr-leeH)* .... naturally
neben *(nay-ben)* .... next to
neblig *(nay-blig)* .... foggy
nehmen *(nay-men)* .... to take
nein *(nine)* .... no
neu, neue, neuen *(noy)(noy-uh)(noy-en)* ...... new
Neujahr, das *(noy-yar)* .... New Year's
neun *(noyn)* ....nine
neunzehn *(noyn-tsayn)* ....nineteen
neunzig *(noyn-tsig)*..................ninety
nicht *(neeHt)* .... no, not
nichts *(neeH-ts)*....................nothing
niedrig *(nee-drig)* .... low
noch *(nohH)* .... still, yet
112 Nord, der *(nort)* ....north

Nordamerika, das *(nort-ah-mair-ih-kah)*........
.... North America
Nordpol, der *(nort-pohl)*............... North Pole
Nordsee, die *(nort-zay)*............. North Sea
Norwegen, das *(nor-vay-gen)* .... Norway
Notausgang, der *(noht-ows-gahng)* . emergency exit
November, der *(noh-vem-bair)* .... November
null *(nool)*...........................zero
Nummer, die *(noo-mair)* ....number
nun *(noon)* .... now

O

oben *(oh-ben)* .... above, upstairs
Obst, das *(ohpst)* .... fruit
Obstgeschäft, das *(ohpst-geh-sheft)*..... fruit store
oder *(oh-dair)* ....or
Ofen, der *(oh-fen)*................... oven
offen *(ohf-fen)* .... open
offiziell *(oh-fee-tsee-el)*..............official
Offizier, der *(oh-fih-tseer)* .... officer
öffnen *(urf-nen)* .... to open
oft *(ohft)* ....often
ohne *(oh-nuh)* ....without
Ohr, das (or) ....ear
Ohrring, der *(or-ring)*............. earring
Oktober, der *(ohk-toh-bair)*........ October
Öl, das *(url)*......................oil
Omelett, das *(oh-meh-let)*...............omelette
Onkel, der *(ohn-kel)* ....uncle
Oper, die *(oh-pair)* .... opera
Opernhaus, das *(oh-pairn-house)*...... opera house
orange *(oh-rahn-zhuh)* ...... orange (color)
Orangensaft, der *(oh-rahn-zhen-zahft)* ..orange juice
Orchester, das *(or-kes-tair)* .... orchestra
Ordnung, die *(ord-noong)* ....order
Organisation, die *(or-gahn-ih-zah-tsee-ohn)* ......
...........................organization
Orgel, die *(or-gel)*................... organ
Österreich, das *(ur-stair-ry-sh)* .... Austria
Ost, der *(ohst)* .... east
Ostern, das *(oh-stairn)* .... Easter
Ostküste, die *(ohst-kews-tuh)* .... east coast
Ozean, der *(oh-tsay-ahn)* .... ocean

P

packen *(pah-ken)*........................ to pack
Paket, das *(pah-kate)* .... package
paniert *(pah-neart)* .... breaded
Papier, das *(pah-peer)* .... paper
Papierkorb, der *(pah-peer-korp)* . wastepaper basket
Park, der *(park)*...................... park
Parkplatz, der *(park-plahts)* .... parking space
parken *(par-ken)* .... to park
Pass, der *(pahss)* .... passport
Passagier, der *(pah-sah-zheer)* .... passenger
Passkontrolle, die *(pahss-kohn-trohl-luh)* ....
.... passport control, check
passen *(pah-sen)* .... to fit
Pension, die *(pahn-see-ohn)* .... guest house
Pfeffer, der *(fef-air)* .... pepper
Pfund, das *(foont)* ....pound
Physik, die *(fih-zeek)*................ physics
Pille, die *(pil-uh)* ....pill

Pizza, die *(pits-zuh)* .... pizza
Platz, der *(plahts)* .... space, place
Polen, das *(poh-len)* .... Poland
Police, die *(poh-lee-suh)* ... policy (insurance)
Politik, die *(poh-lih-teek)* .... politics
Polizei, die *(poh-lih-tsy)* .... police
Polnisch, das *(pohl-nish)* .... Polish (language)
Portugal, das *(por-too-gahl)* .... Portugal
Portugiesisch, das *(por-too-gee-zish)* ... Portuguese
Post, die *(post)* .... mail
Postamt, das *(post-ahmt)* .... post office
Postkarte, die *(pohst-kar-tuh)* .... postcard
Preis, der *(price)* .... price
Priester, der *(pree-stair)* .... priest
Problem, das *(pro-blame)* .... problem
Programm, das *(pro-grahm)* .... program
progressiv *(pro-gres-seev)* .... progressive
Pulli, der *(poo-lee)* .... sweater
purpur *(poor-poor)* .... purple

Q

Qualität, die *(kvah-lih-tate)* .... quality
Quantität, die *(kvahn-tih-tate)* .... quantity
Quittung, die *(kvih-toong)* .... receipt

R

radikal *(rah-dee-kahl)* .... radical
Radio, das *(rah-dee-oh)* .... radio
Rathaus, das *(raht-house)* .... city hall
Ratskeller, der *(rahts-kel-air)* ...city-hall restaurant
Rasiermesser, das *(rah-zeer-mes-air)* .... razor
Rechnung, die *(rehH-noong)* .... bill
recht *(rehHt)* .... right, correct
rechts *(rehH-ts)* .... right
Regenmantel, der *(ray-gen-mahn-tel)* .... raincoat
Regenschirm, der *(ray-gen-shirm)* ...... umbrella
Regiobahn (RB), die *(ray-gee-oh-bahn)* ....
.... local train service
Regioexpress (RE), die *(ray-gee-oh-eks-press)* ....
.... local express train service
regnen *(rayg-nen)* .... to rain
reich *(ry-sh)* .... rich
Reinigung, die *(ry-nih-goong)* .....dry cleaners
Reise, die *(ry-zuh)* .... trip, travel
Reisebüro, das *(ry-zuh-bew-roh)* ...... travel office
reisen *(ry-zen)* .... to travel
Reisende, der *(ry-zen-duh)* .... traveler
Reisechecks, die *(ry-zuh-shecks)* .traveler's checks
Religion, die *(ray-lee-gee-ohn)* ....religion
Republik, die *(ray-poo-bleek)* .... republic
reservieren *(rez-air-veer-en)* ....to reserve
Reservierung, die *(rez-air-veer-oong)* .. reservation
Residenz, die *(ray-zih-dents)* .... residence
Restaurant, das *(res-toh-rahnt)* .... restaurant
Rettungsdienst, der *(ret-toongs-deenst)*. rescue service
Richter, der *(reeH-tair)* .... judge
richtig *(reeH-teeg)* .... correct
Ring, der *(ring)* .... ring
Risiko, das *(ree-zee-koh)* .... risk
Ritter, der *(rit-tair)* .... knight
Rock, der *(rohk)* .... skirt
rosa *(roh-zah)* ....pink
Rose, die *(roh-zuh)* ....rose
rot *(roht)* .... red

Ruine, die *(roo-ee-nuh)* .... ruins
Rumänien, das *(roo-may-nee-en)* ....Romania
rund *(roont)* .... round
Russisch, das *(roo-sish)* .....Russian (language)
Russland, das *(roos-lahnt)* ....Russia

S

S-Bahn, die *(s-bahn)* .... streetcar
sagen *(zah-gen)* .... to say
Salat, der *(zah-laht)* ....salad
Salz, das *(zahlts)* .... salt
Samstag, der *(zahms-tahk)* .... Saturday
Sandalen, die *(zahn-dah-len)* .... sandals
sauber *(zow-bair)* .... clean
sauer *(zow-air)* ....sour
Schalter, der *(shahl-tair)* ....counter
scharf *(sharf)* .... sharp, spicy
Scheck, der *(sheck)* .... check
Schein, der *(shine)* .... bank note, bill
schicken *(shick-en)* .... to send
Schiff, das *(shif)* .... ship
Schinken, der *(shink-en)* ....ham
Schlafanzug, der *(shlahf-ahn-tsook)* ...... pajamas
schlafen *(shlah-fen)* .... to sleep
Schlafwagen, der *(shlahf-vah-gen)* ..... sleeping car
Schlafzimmer, das *(shlahf-tsih-mair)* .....bedroom
Schlagsahne, die *(shlahg-zah-nuh)* . whipped cream
schlecht *(shlehHt)* .... bad
schließen *(shlee-sen)* .... to close
Schloss, das *(shlohss)* .... castle
schneien *(shny-en)* .... to snow
schnell *(shnel)* .... fast
Schnellimbiss, der *(shnel-im-biss)*. refreshment bar
Schokolade, die *(shoh-koh-lah-duh)* ..... chocolate
schön *(shurn)* .... pretty
Schottland, das *(shoht-lahnt)* ....Scotland
Schrank, der *(shrahnk)* ...... closet, cupboard
schreiben *(shry-ben)* ....to write
Schreibtisch, der *(shripe-tish)* .... desk
Schreibwarengeschäft, das *(shripe-var-en-geh-sheft)*
...............................stationery store
Schuhe, die *(shoo-uh)* ....shoes
Schule, die *(shoo-luh)* .... school
schwarz *(shvarts)* ....black
Schweden, das *(shvay-den)* ....Sweden
Schwedisch, das *(shvay-dish)* .. Swedish (language)
Schweiz, die *(shvites)* .... Switzerland
schwer *(shvair)* ....difficult, hard
Schwester, die *(shves-tair)* ....sister
schwimmen *(shvim-men)* ....to swim
sechs *(zeks)* .... six
sechzehn *(zeks-tsayn)* .... sixteen
sechzig *(zek-tsig)* .... sixty
See, die *(zay)* ....sea
sehen *(zay-en)* .... to see
sehr *(zair)* .... very
Seife, die *(zy-fuh)* .... soap
Seite, die *(zy-tuh)* .... page
Sekunde, die *(zay-koon-duh)* .... second
September, der *(zep-tem-bair)* ....September
Serviette, die *(zair-vee-et-tuh)* .... napkin
Shorts, die *(shorts)* .... shorts
sie *(zee)* ....she, they
Sie *(zee)* .... you

113

sieben *(zee-ben)* . . . . seven
siebzehn *(zeep-tsayn)* . . . . seventeen
siebzig *(zeep-tsig)* . . . . seventy
Silvester, der *(sil-ves-tair)* . . . . New Year's Eve
sind *(zint)* . . . . they, we, you are
singen *(zing-en)* . . . . to sing
sitzen *(zit-tsen)* . . . . to sit
Ski, der *(she)* . . . . ski
Slowakei, die *(sloh-vah-ky)* . . . . Slovakia
so . . . wie *(zoh) (vee)* . . . . as . . . as
Socken, die *(zoh-ken)* . . . . socks
Sofa, das *(soh-fah)* . . . . sofa
Sohn, der *(zohn)* . . . . son
Sommer, der *(zoh-mair)* . . . . summer
Sonne, die *(zoh-nuh)* . . . . sun
Sonnenbrille, die *(zoh-nen-bril-luh)* . . . . sunglasses
Sonntag, der *(zohn-tahk)* . . . . Sunday
Spanien, das *(shpah-nee-en)* . . . . Spain
Spanisch, das *(shpah-nish)* . . . . . Spanish (language)
spät *(shpay-t)* . . . . late
Speise, die *(shpy-zuh)* . . . . food
Speisekarte, die *(shpy-zuh-kar-tuh)* . . . . menu
Speisewagen, der *(shpy-zuh-vah-gen)* . . . . dining car
Spezialität, die *(shpay-tsee-ah-lih-tate)* . . . specialty
Spiegel, der *(shpee-gel)* . . . . mirror
Sport, der *(shport)* . . . . sport
sprechen *(shpreh-Hen)* . . . . to speak
Staat, der *(shtaht)* . . . . state, country
Stadt, die *(shtaht)* . . . . city
Stadtmitte, die *(shtaht-mit-tuh)* . . . . city center
Stadtplan, der *(shtaht-plahn)* . . . . city map
Stiefel, die *(shtee-fel)* . . . . boots
Stock, das *(shtohk)* . . . . floor
Straße, die *(shtrah-suh)* . . . . street
Straßenbahn, die *(shtrah-sen-bahn)* . . . . . streetcar
Straßenbahnhaltestelle, die *(shtrah-sen-bahn-hahl-tuh-shtel-luh)* . . . . streetcar stop
Strumpfhose, die *(shtroomf-hoh-zuh)* . . . panty hose
Stück, das *(shtewk)* . . . . piece
Student, der *(shtoo-dent)* . . . . student (male)
Studentin, die *(shtoo-dent-in)* . . . . . student (female)
Stuhl, der *(shtool)* . . . . chair
Stunde, die *(shtoon-duh)* . . . . hour
Sturm, der *(shturm)* . . . . storm
Süd *(zewt)* . . . . south
Südafrika, das *(zewt-ah-frih-kah)* . . . . South Africa
Südamerika, das *(zewt-ah-mair-ih-kah)* . . . . South America
Südpol, der *(zewt-pohl)* . . . . South Pole
Supermarkt, der *(zoo-pair-markt)* . . . . supermarket
Suppe, die *(zoo-puh)* . . . . soup
süß *(zoos)* . . . . sweet
Symphonie, die *(zoom-foh-nee)* . . . . symphony

T

Tabakladen, der *(tah-bahk-lah-den)* . . tobacco store
Tag, der *(tahk)* . . . . day
Tagesgericht, das *(tah-ges-geh-reeHt)* . . . . daily meal special
Tankstelle, die *(tahnk-shtel-luh)* . . . . gas station
Tante, die *(tahn-tuh)* . . . . aunt
Tanz, der *(tahn-ts)* . . . . dance
tanzen *(tahn-tsen)* . . . . to dance
Taschentuch, das *(tah-shen-tooH)* . . . . handkerchief
Tasse, die *(tah-suh)* . . . . cup

tausend *(tau-zent)* . . . . thousand
Taxi, das *(tahk-see)* . . . . taxi
Tee, der *(tay)* . . . . tea
Telefon, das *(tay-lay-fohn)* . . . . telephone
Telefonanruf, der *(tay-lay-fohn-ahn-roof)* . . . . telephone call
Telefonbuch, das *(tay-lay-fohn-booH)* . . . . telephone book
Telefongespräch, das *(tay-lay-fohn-geh-shprayH)* . . . . telephone conversation
telefonieren *(tay-lay-foh-neer-en)* . . . . . to telephone
Telefonistin, die *(tay-lay-foh-nee-stin)* . . . . operator
Telefonkarte, die *(tay-lay-fohn-kar-tuh)* . . . . telephone card
Telefonzelle, die *(tay-lay-fohn-tsel-luh)* . . . . telephone booth
Teller, der *(tel-air)* . . . . plate
Temperatur, die *(tem-pair-ah-toor)* . . . temperature
Tennisschuhe, die *(ten-is-shoo-uh)* . . . . tennis shoes
Teppich, der *(tep-eeH)* . . . . carpet
teuer *(toy-air)* . . . . expensive
Theaterkarte, die *(tay-ah-tair-kar-tuh)* . theater ticket
Thermometer, das *(tair-moh-may-tair)* . thermometer
Tisch, der *(tish)* . . . . table
Tochter, die *(tohH-tair)* . . . . daughter
Toilette, die *(toy-let-tuh)* . . . . lavatory
Tomatensaft, der *(toh-mah-ten-zahft)* . . tomato juice
träumen *(troy-men)* . . . . to dream
trinken *(trink-en)* . . . . to drink
Trinkgeld, das *(trink-gelt)* . . . . tip
Tschüs! *(choos)* . . . . good-bye
T-Shirt, das *(tee-shirt)* . . . . t-shirt
Tuch, das *(tooH)* . . . . towel
tun *(toon)* . . . . to do
Tür, die *(tewr)* . . . . door
typische *(too-pish-uh)* . . . . typical

U

U-Bahn, die *(oo-bahn)* . . . . subway
U-Bahnhaltestelle, die *(oo-bahn-hahl-tuh-shtel-luh)* . . . . subway stop
U-Bahnkarte, die *(oo-bahn-kar-tuh)* . subway ticket
über *(ew-bair)* . . . . over, above
Uhr, die *(oor)* . . . . clock, watch
um *(oom)* . . . . around, at
umsteigen *(oom-shty-gen)* . . . . to transfer
und *(oont)* . . . . and
Ungarn, das *(oon-garn)* . . . . Hungary
Ungarisch, das *(oon-gar-ish)* . . . Hungarian (language)
ungefähr *(oon-geh-fair)* . . . . approximately
uninteressant *(oon-in-tair-es-sahnt)* . . uninteresting
Uniform, die *(oo-nee-form)* . . . . uniform
Universität, die *(oo-nih-vair-zih-tate)* . . . . university
unten *(oon-ten)* . . . . below, downstairs
unter *(oon-tair)* . . . . under
Untergrund, der *(oon-tair-groont)* . . . . subway
Unterhemd, das *(oon-tair-hemt)* . . . . undershirt
Unterhose, die *(oon-tair-hoh-zuh)* . . . . . underpants
Unterrock, der *(oon-tair-rohk)* . . . . slip
unterwegs *(oon-tair-vehgs)* . . . in transit, on the way
Unterwelt, die *(oon-tair-velt)* . . . . underworld

V

Vater, der *(fah-tair)* . . . . father
Verb, das *(vairb)* . . . . verb

114

Verbindung, die (fair-bin-doong) . . . . . . connection
verboten (fair-boh-ten) . . . . prohibited
Vereinigten Staaten, die (fair-eye-neeg-ten)(shtah-ten)
. . . . the United States
verkaufen (fair-kow-fen) . . . . to sell
verlieren (fair-lear-en) . . . . to lose
verstehen (fair-shtay-en) . . . . to understand
Verzeihung (fair-tsy-oong) . . . . excuse me
viel (feel) . . . . much, a lot
viel Glück (feel)(glewk) . . . . much luck,
viel Spaß (feel)(shpahs) . . . . much fun
vier (fear) . . . . four
Viertel, das (fear-tel) . . . . quarter
vierzehn (fear-tsayn) . . . . fourteen
vierzig (fear-tsig) . . . . forty
violett (vee-oh-let) . . . . violet
voll (fohl) . . . . full, drunk
Volk, das (folk) . . . . folk, people
vom (=von dem) . . . . from the
vom Kalb (fohm)(kahlp) . . . . veal
vom Lamm (fohm)(lahm) . . . . lamb
vom Rind (fohm)(rint) . . . . beef
vom Schwein (fohm)(shvine) . . . . pork
von (fohn) . . . . from
vor (for) . . . . in front of
Vorfahrt, die (for-fahrt) . . . . right-of-way
Vorhang, der (for-hahng) . . . . curtain
Vorname, der (for-nah-muh) . . . . first name
Vorspeisen, die (for-shpy-zen) . . . . appetizers

W

Wagen, der (vah-gen) . . . . car
wandern (vahn-dairn) . . . . . . to wander, hike
wann (vahn) . . . . when
war (var) . . . . was
Waren, die (var-en) . . . . wares
warm (varm) . . . . warm
Warnung, die (var-noong) . . . . warning
Wartesaal, der (var-tuh-zahl) . . . . waiting room
warum (vah-room) . . . . why
was (vahs) . . . . what
Waschbecken, das (vahsh-beck-en) . . . . sink
waschen (vah-shen) . . . . to wash
Wäscherei, die (vesh-air-eye) . . . . laundry
Wasser, das (vah-sair) . . . . water
Wechselstube, die (veck-zel-shtoo-buh) . . . .
. . . . money-exchange office
Wecker, der (veck-air) . . . . alarm clock
Weg, der (veg) . . . . way
Wein, der (vine) . . . . wine
Weihnachten, die (vy-nahH-ten) . . . . . Christmas
Weihnachtsgeschenke, die (vy-nahHts-geh-shen-kuh)
. . . . Christmas presents
Weinglas, das (wine-glahs) . . . . wine glass
Weinstube, die (vine-shtoo-buh) . . . . wine cellar
weiß (vice) . . . . white
weiß (vice) . . . . he, she, it knows
Weißwein, der (vice-vine) . . . . white wine
weiter (vy-tair) . . . . further
welche, welches (vel-chuh)(vel-ches) . . . . . which
wenig (vay-nig) . . . . few
wer (vair) . . . . who

Westküste, die (vest-kews-tuh) . . . . . . west coast
Westen, der (ves-ten) . . . . west
Westfälisch (vest-fay-lish) . . . . Westphalian (region)
Wetter, das (vet-tair) . . . . weather
wichtig (veeH-teeg) . . . . important
wie (vee) . . . . how
Wie geht es Ihnen? (vee)(gate)(es)(ee-nen) . . . . . .
. . . . How are you?
wieder (vee-dair) . . . . again
wiederholen (vee-dair-hoh-len) . . . . to repeat
wie viel (vee)(feel) . . . . how much
wie viele (vee)(fee-luh) . . . . how many
Wild, das (vilt) . . . . venison, game
Willkommen, das (vil-koh-men) . . . . welcome
Wind, der (vint) . . . . wind
windig (vin-dig) . . . . windy
Winter, der (vin-tair) . . . . winter
wir (veer) . . . . we
wissen (viss-en) . . . . to know (a fact)
wo (voh) . . . . where
Woche, die (voh-Huh) . . . . week
wohl (vohl) . . . . well
wohnen (voh-nen) . . . . to live, reside
Wohnzimmer, das (vohn-tsih-mair) . . . . living room
Wolle, der (voh-luh) . . . . wool
Wort, das (vort) . . . . word
Wörter, die (vur-tair) . . . . words
Wörterbuch, das (vur-tair-booH) . . . . dictionary
wünschen (vewn-shen) . . . . to wish
Wurst, die (vurst) . . . . sausage

Z

Zahnbürste, die (tsahn-bewr-stuh) . . . . . toothbrush
Zahnpasta, die (tsahn-pah-stah) . . . . . . toothpaste
zehn (tsayn) . . . . ten
Zentimeter, der (tsen-tih-may-tair) . . . . . centimeter
zeigen (tsy-gen) . . . . to show
Zeitschrift, die (tsight-shrift) . . . . magazine
Zeitung, die (tsy-toong) . . . . newspaper
Zentimeter, der (tsen-tih-may-tair) . . . . . centimeter
Zentrum, das (tsen-troom) . . . . . center (of a city)
Zeremonie, die (tsair-eh-moh-nee) . . . . ceremony
ziehen (tsee-en) . . . . to pull (doors)
Zigarre, die (tsih-gah-ruh) . . . . cigar
Zigarette, die (tsih-gah-ret-tuh) . . . . cigarette
Zimmer, das (tsih-mair) . . . . room
Zirkus, der (tseer-koos) . . . . circus
Zivilisation, die (tsih-vih-lih-zah-tsee-ohn) . . . .
. . . . civilization
Zoll, der (tsohl) . . . . customs
Zoo, der (tsoh) . . . . zoo
zu (tsoo) . . . . closed, to, too
Zucker, der (tsoo-kair) . . . . sugar
zu (tsoo) . . . . to, closed
Zug, der (tsook) . . . . train
Züge, die (tsue-guh) . . . . trains
zum (= zu dem) . . . . to the
zur (= zu der) . . . . to the
zusammen (tsoo-zah-men) . . . . together
zwanzig (tsvahn-tsig) . . . . twenty
zwei (tsvy) . . . . two
zweihundert (tsvy-hoon-dairt) . . . . . . two hundred
zweiter (tsvy-tair) . . . . second
zwischen (tsvih-shen) . . . . between
zwölf (ts-vurlf) . . . . twelve

This beverage guide is intended to explain the variety of beverages available to you while **in Deutschland oder** any other German-speaking country. It is by no means complete. Some of the experimenting has been left up to you, but this should get you started.

HEIßE GETRÄNKE (hot drinks)

Tasse Kaffee	cup of coffee
Kännchen Kaffee	small pot of coffee
Glas Tee	cup of tea
Kännchen Tee	small pot of tea
mit Zitrone	with lemon
mit Sahne	with cream
mit Milch	with milk

KALTE GETRÄNKE (cold drinks)

Spezi	½ cola, ½ Fanta
Apfelsaft	apple juice
Orangensaft	orange juice
Tomatensaft	tomato juice
Milch	milk
Orangenlimonade	orange drink
Zitronenlimonade	lemon-flavored drink
Mineralwasser	mineral water
mit Kohlensäure	carbonated
ohne Kohlensäure	non-carbonated
Apfelsaftschorle	apple juice and mineral water

SPIRITUOSEN (spirits)

Gin	gin
Rum	rum
Russischer Wodka	Russian vodka
Kirschwasser	cherry schnapps
Himbeergeist	raspberry schnapps
Williams-Birne	pear schnapps

APÉRITIFS (aperitifs)

Sherry	sherry
Portwein	port

BIERE (beers)

Bier is purchased in **Flaschen** (bottles) or **vom Faß** (draft).

Export vom Faß	draft export
Pils	pilsner
Diät-Pils	lite pilsner
Altbier	dark beer
Weizenbier	special wheat beer
Berliner Weiße	Berlin specialty —
(mit oder ohne	(with or without
Schuß-Waldmeister	a shot of Waldmeister
oder Himbeersirup)	or raspberry syrup)

WEINE (wines)

Wein is purchased by the **Flasche** (bottle) or **offen** (open, like a house wine).

Rotwein	red wine
Weißwein	white wine
Rosé	rosé
Tafelwein	table wine
Qualitätswein	quality wine
Kabinettwein	choice wine
Eiswein	ice wine (rare)
Schorle	wine mixed with mineral water

LIKÖRE (liqueurs)

Eierlikör	egg liqueur
Kirschlikör	cherry liqueur

GUT IM SOMMER

Erdbeerbowle	champagne, white wine, strawberries
Pfirsichbowle	champagne, white wine, peaches

GUT IM WINTER

Feuerzangenbowle	red wine, orange slices, spices, sugar block coated with rum, flambé

(eeH)
ich

(veer)
wir

(air)
er

(zee)
Sie

(zee)
sie

(es)
es

(koh-men)
kommen
(koh-muh)
ich komme

(gay-en)
gehen
(gay-uh)
ich gehe

(hah-ben)
haben
(hah-buh)
ich habe

(lair-nen)
lernen
(lair-nuh)
ich lerne

(brow-Hen)
brauchen
(brow-Huh)
ich brauche

(murk-ten)
möchten
(murk-tuh)
ich möchte

we	I
you	he
it	she / they
to go	to come
I go	I come
to learn	to have
I learn	I have
would like	to need
I would like	I need

(kow-fen) **kaufen** *(kow-fuh)* **ich kaufe**	*(beh-shtel-len)* **bestellen** *(beh-shtel-luh)* **ich bestelle**
(voh-nen) **wohnen** *(voh-nuh)* **ich wohne**	*(bly-ben)* **bleiben** *(bly-buh)* **ich bleibe**
(shpreh-Hen) **sprechen** *(shpreh-Huh)* **ich spreche**	*(hi-sen)* **heißen** *(hi-suh)* **ich heiße**
(ess-en) **essen** *(ess-uh)* **ich esse**	*(trink-en)* **trinken** *(trink-uh)* **ich trinke**
(zah-gen) **sagen** *(zah-guh)* **ich sage**	*(fair-shtay-en)* **verstehen** *(fair-shtay-uh)* **ich verstehe**
(fair-kow-fen) **verkaufen** *(fair-kow-fuh)* **ich verkaufe**	*(vee-dair-hoh-len)* **wiederholen** *(vee-dair-hoh-luh)* **ich wiederhole**

CUT ALONG DOTTED LINE, FOLD AND TAKE WITH YOU

to order	to buy
I order	I buy
to remain / stay	to live / reside
I remain / stay	I live / reside
to be called	to speak
I am called / my name is	I speak
to drink	to eat
I drink	I eat
to understand	to say
I understand	I say
to repeat	to sell
I repeat	I sell

(fin-den)
finden
(fin-duh)
ich finde

(zay-en)
sehen
(zay-uh)
ich sehe

(shick-en)
schicken
(shick-uh)
ich schicke

(shlah-fen)
schlafen
(shlah-fuh)
ich schlafe

(mah-Hen)
machen
(mah-Huh)
ich mache

(beh-tsah-len)
bezahlen
(beh-tsah-luh)
ich bezahle

(tsy-gen)
zeigen
(tsy-guh)
ich zeige

(shry-ben)
schreiben
(shry-buh)
ich schreibe

(lay-zen)
lesen
(lay-zuh)
ich lese

(kur-nen)
können
(kahn)
ich kann

(mew-sen)
müssen
(moos)
ich muss

(viss-en)
wissen
(vice)
ich weiß

to see	to find
I see	I find
to sleep	to send
I sleep	I send
to pay	to make / do
I pay	I make / do
to write	to show
I write	I show
to be able to / can	to read
I can	I read
to know (fact)	to have to / must
I know	I have to / must

(ahp-fah-ren)
abfahren
(tsook) *(fairt)* *(ahp)*
der Zug fährt ab

(flee-gen)
fliegen
(flee-guh)
ich fliege

(ry-zen)
reisen
(ry-zuh)
ich reise

(ahn-koh-men)
ankommen
(tsook) *(kohmt)* *(ahn)*
der Zug kommt an

(fah-ren)
fahren
(fah-ruh)
ich fahre

(oom-shty-gen)
umsteigen
(shty-guh) *(oom)*
ich steige um

(pah-ken)
packen
(pah-kuh)
ich packe

(zit-tsen)
sitzen
(zit-tsuh)
ich sitze

(gipt)
es gibt

(vah-shen)
waschen
(vah-shuh)
ich wasche

(gay-ben) *(zee)* *(mir)*
Geben Sie mir . . .

(fair-lear-en)
verlieren
(fair-lear-uh)
ich verliere

to fly	to depart
I fly	the train departs
to arrive	to travel
the train arrives	I travel
to transfer	to drive, travel by vehicle
I transfer	I drive
to sit	to pack
I sit	I pack
to wash	there is / there are
I wash	
to lose	give me . . .
I lose	

(hoy -tuh)	*(vee)* *(gate)* *(es)* *(ee-nen)*
heute	**Wie geht es Ihnen?**

(ges-tairn)	*(bit-tuh)*
gestern	**bitte**

(mor-gen)	*(dahn-kuh)*
morgen	**danke**

(owf) *(vee-dair-zay-en)*	*(ent-shool-dee-goong)*
Auf Wiedersehen!	**Entschuldigung**

(ahlt) *(noy)*	*(vee)* *(feel)* *(koh-stet)* *(dahs)*
alt - neu	**Wie viel kostet das?**

(grohs) *(kline)*	*(owf)* *(tsoo)*
groß - klein	**auf - zu**

How are you?	today
please	yesterday
thank you	tomorrow
excuse me	good-bye
How much does that cost?	old - new
open - closed	large / tall - small / short

(geh-zoont) *(krahnk)*
gesund - krank

(goot) *(shlehHt)*
gut - schlecht

(hice) *(kahlt)*
heiß - kalt

(koorts) *(lahng)*
kurz - lang

(hohH) *(nee-drig)*
hoch - niedrig

(oh-ben) *(oon-ten)*
oben - unten

(links) *(rehH-ts)*
links - rechts

(lahng-zahm) *(shnel)*
langsam - schnell

(ahlt) *(yoong)*
alt - jung

(toy-air) *(bil-lig)*
teuer - billig

(arm) *(ry-sh)*
arm - reich

(feel) *(vay-nig)*
viel - wenig

good - bad   healthy - sick

short - long   hot - cold

above - below   high - low

slow - fast   left - right

expensive-
inexpensive   old - young

a lot - a little   poor - rich

Now that you've finished...

You've done it!

You've completed all the Steps, stuck your labels, flashed your cards, cut out your beverage and menu guides and practiced your new language. Do you realize how far you've come and how much you've learned? You've accomplished what it could take years to achieve in a traditional language class.

You can now confidently

- ask questions,
- understand directions,
- make reservations,
- order food and
- shop for anything.

And you can do it all in a foreign language! Go anywhere with confidence — from a large cosmopolitan restaurant to a small, out-of-the-way village where no one speaks English. Your experiences will be much more enjoyable and worry-free now that you speak the language.

As you've seen, learning a foreign language can be fun. Why limit yourself to just one? Now you're ready to learn another language with the *10 minutes a day*® Series!

Kris Kershul

Kristine Kershul

To place an order –

- Visit us at **www.bbks.com**, day or night.
- Call us at (800) 488-5068 or (206) 284-4211 between 8:00 a.m. and 5:00 p.m. Pacific Time, Monday - Friday.
- If you have questions about ordering, please call us. You may also fax us at (206) 284-3660 or email us at customer.service@bbks.com.

132